BLUEPRINTS

Maths
Assessment
Key Stage 1

David and Wendy Clemson

Stanley Thornes (Publishers) Ltd

Do you receive BLUEPRINTS NEWS?

Blueprints is an expanding series of practical teacher's ideas books and photocopiable resources for use in primary schools. Books are available for separate infant and junior age ranges for every core and foundation subject, as well as for an ever widening range of other primary teaching needs. These include **Blueprints Primary English** books and **Blueprints Resource Banks**. **Blueprints** are carefully structured around the demands of the National Curriculum in England and Wales, but are used successfully by schools and teachers in Scotland, Northern Ireland and elsewhere.

Blueprints provide:

- *Total curriculum coverage*
- *Hundreds of practical ideas*
- *Books specifically for the age range you teach*
- *Flexible resources for the whole school or for individual teachers*
- *Excellent photocopiable sheets – ideal for assessment and children's work profiles*
- *Supreme value.*

Books may be bought by credit card over the telephone and information obtained on **(01242) 577944**. Alternatively, photocopy and return this **FREEPOST** form to receive **Blueprints News**, our regular update on all new and existing titles. You may also like to add the name of a friend who would be interested in being on the mailing list.

Please add my name to the **BLUEPRINTS NEWS** mailing list.

Mr/Mrs/Miss/Ms _____

Home address _____

_____ Postcode _____

School address _____

_____ Postcode _____

Please also send **BLUEPRINTS NEWS** to:

Mr/Mrs/Miss/Ms _____

Address _____

_____ Postcode _____

To: Marketing Services Dept., Stanley Thornes Ltd, FREEPOST (GR 782), Cheltenham, GL50 1BR

First published in 1995 by:
Stanley Thornes (Publishers) Ltd
Ellenborough House
Wellington Street
CHELTENHAM GL50 1YW

96 97 98 99 00 / 10 9 8 7 6 5 4 3 2

A catalogue record for this book is available from the British Library.

0 7487 1751 X

Typeset by John Youé Design, Honiton, Devon
Printed and bound in Great Britain

Contents

Introduction

An important part of a teacher's work is the constant assessment of children's learning. Only by assessing can we devise what children should do next and give them tasks that are appropriate. It is to support teachers in their assessment of children's work in mathematics that this book has been written. The book begins with some pointers to the methods of collecting assessment information that are available to teachers. These and the assessment tasks that follow are intended to support teachers in forming their own assessments of what children know and can do. The exercises are not intended as rigorous in-depth 'tests'. Rather, they are indicators or clues to where the children have reached, and we see them as having a predominantly formative purpose.

We have deliberately made the assessment exercises as varied as possible for two reasons: firstly, so that teachers can use a variety of everyday classroom settings to glean assessment information; secondly, we believe a variety of activities motivates children and enables them to better demonstrate their mastery of mathematics.

BLUEPRINTS MATHS ASSESSMENT AND THE NATIONAL CURRICULUM

Blueprints Maths Assessment is a practical teacher's resource specifically tied in to the requirements of the National Curriculum for mathematics in primary schools. It offers assessment tasks which teachers can use alongside those they devise themselves, or with more formal 'tests'. *Blueprints Maths Assessment: Key Stage 1* provides tasks for children between 5 and 7 years old; *Blueprints Maths Assessment: Key Stage 2* provides tasks for children between 7 and 11 years old. Teacher's notes and assessment copymasters are combined in one book for each Key Stage. The sequence the exercises follow matches that of the content of *Mathematics in the National Curriculum (1995).*

Blueprints Maths Assessment: Key Stage 1 provides a set of assessment tasks through Key Stage 1. The assessment exercises are arranged in three sections, each related to the assessment of work expected of children through this Key Stage: Attainment Targets 1, 2 and 3, at Levels 1–3.

Because all three parts of the programme of study – using and applying mathematics, number and algebra, and shape, space and measures – are interrelated, work in one area can be used to assess understanding in another. The settings in which we have chosen to place assessment tasks are exemplars. Teachers can use the tasks given in flexible ways. For example, Task 3 in Attainment Target 1 could be used to determine a Level 1 performance in either Attainment Target 1 or Attainment Target 2.

At the start of the teacher's notes about the assessment tasks relating to each Level of each Attainment Target there is an extract from the Statutory Orders, comprising the Attainment Target title, and the appropriate Level description. Attached to each assessment task is a copymaster. In some cases the copymaster is for the teacher's use and in others for the children's use. This assessment copymaster is labelled 'A'. For all tasks there are also reassessment copymasters, labelled 'B'. Each of these appears immediately after each 'first try' copymaster. Here are some ways of using the reassessment ideas:

- for children to do as an addition to the first assessment task
- where children make mistakes on the first task, as a second try at a later date
- where a group of children are doing the task at the same time some can be given the assessment version and some the reassessment version

There are two summary record sheets at the back of the book. The first is a tick list to enable you to record which children in the class have done each task at a specific Level. The second is a tick list that can be kept for each child, showing those tasks the child has tried and which of them successfully.

RECORD KEEPING

There are photocopiable record sheets at the back of the book. Photocopy one Record Sheet 1 per class to maintain a tick list to show assessment tasks tried at a specific Level. Photocopy one Record Sheet 2 per child and tick the assessment tasks tried, those done successfully, and reassessment attempts where appropriate. This record sheet can be added to school records.

Methods for Collecting Assessment Information

There are five ways in which teachers can collect assessment information:

- observing
- listening
- participating
- scrutinizing written outcomes
- giving tests

To carry through assessment effectively, using any of these methods for collecting information, demands expertise that is sometimes not acknowledged. To alert you to some of the important issues to think about when choosing and using assessment methods, the following will be listed for each method:

- how to do it
- advantages
- disadvantages

OBSERVING

Teachers constantly monitor the work of a whole class and maintain an overview. While something you notice by chance can, of course, contribute to your assessments, observations need to be more deliberate in order to be systematic. You cannot expect to 'notice' all you need to see on days when you are working with the whole class. To allow you to observe, it is therefore important that there is another adult present to whom the children can turn.

Set yourself a focussed brief. A general aim may not allow you to collect usable information. Take chronological notes, which will remind you of the flow of events you observed.

Make interpretations of your notes for the record as soon as you can after the session to avoid having to recall from distant memory what exactly went on.

ADVANTAGES   Observations can yield a variety of information in one session. Observations can be made of a number of children working alongside one another or cooperatively. Children can be observed in the course of their 'normal' school day.

DISADVANTAGES   If you have planned to observe while you monitor the whole class, your time for observation will probably be brief or sporadic. Another adult in the room would, of course, free you to observe for longer periods. The information is unpredictable, and what you hoped to observe may not happen because of the dynamic of the classroom that day.

LISTENING

Assessment information you have heard can be collected in a variety of classroom settings. You can listen to a group involved in a collaborative activity, or when they are setting up or clearing away. You can tape-record such sessions and glean assessment information by listening to the tape after school is over. You can assess by listening when you give a child individual attention. Good opportunities for assessing by listening also occur when the children are an audience to which individuals have a chance to speak.

You can help to focus the topics talked about, so that sometimes they talk about some mathematical information they have collected, how they have set down their maths work in their books, how they solved a number mystery and so on.

An additional important source of assessment information is what we hear by chance. This information is as potent as any other but needs supplementing with systematically collected information, perhaps sometimes with the help of another adult.

ADVANTAGES   Listening to assess can be done, like observing, during the course of a 'normal' school day. A tape recording can augment your notes.

DISADVANTAGES   There is a temptation to direct conversations and prompt children to follow your agenda and not their own (which would threaten the validity of assessments). Your own interpretions of what children have said may not always coincide with what they intended to convey, and, if you say, 'what did you mean?' or 'is this what you meant?' you may intimidate a child who wants to please you.

PARTICIPATING

When you join in with what children are doing you can not only catalyse and provoke their thinking, but also probe their thinking processes in ways that may prove impossible using other assessment collection methods. However, inevitably, when you join in an activity, the children change what they do and how they respond to the task. Thus the information you get may give more insights into how the children are working, but you have had a greater influence on what happened.

We cannot say children can do some aspect of mathematical work if they always need help, even if it is just the occasional question like, for example, 'What do you do next?', 'Where does that three go?' or 'I'd look at the one you have just done if I were you'. Thus you have to be circumspect about assessments made on the sole basis of information gathered while you are participating in the task.

ADVANTAGES   It may well involve you in behaving just as you do at any other time in class, and you can be yourself. It can be more rewarding for you, the assessor, than trying to maintain a distance from the children you are assessing.

DISADVANTAGES   You cannot record any notes at the time. Focusing your assessment while involved in the dynamic of conversation and action can be difficult. Assessments are probably less problematic if the teacher is not involved, so perhaps participating should not be a first-choice method for getting assessment information.

SCRUTINIZING WRITTEN OUTCOMES
By this we do not mean marking, though it may be part of the process of assessment. The idea of a written examination as a way of demonstrating achievement probably affects how everyone, including children, parents and teachers, feel about what they put on paper. It is regarded as the primary source of learning evidence. It can indeed give indicators about recording skills and understanding of a necessary sequence of steps in mathematical operations. For much of the learning that children do in the infant school, however, the other ways of collecting assessment information are more potent in determining children's *understanding* of mathematics.

ADVANTAGES   You can actually do the assessing with a child while they sit alongside you in class. It can be very important in letting children know about the standards you apply. It can also help to show children how they themselves can determine what their best is. You can also assess children's work outside the school day. The assessment information is complete and concrete, and available for review. This whole record of information and interpretations can be stored as a part of the child's progress record or portfolio.

DISADVANTAGES   What is written down tells you little about whether the child understands the work done. There can be aspects of written work which threaten to contaminate our judgements. For example, we may judge neatly presented work as better than less-tidy work, whether or not it matches the standard of less-tidy work in terms of content.

GIVING TESTS
This is an important method of collecting assessment information throughout the education system. However, it has little place in this book, for we do not view the tasks we have devised as being tests in the strictest sense. They are intended rather as indicators to support teachers' own judgements. Teachers may, however, wish to support their assessments by selecting a few tasks and assembling them into a 'home-made' test across Attainment Targets or Levels for individuals or groups of children. The advantages and disadvantages of giving tests are legion, and beyond the scope of this book.

FURTHER READING
Clemson, D and W Clemson, *The Really Practical Guide to Primary Assessment*, Stanley Thornes, 1991
Clemson, D and W Clemson, *Mathematics in the Early Years,* Routledge, 1994
Duncan, A and W Dunn, *What Primary Teachers Should Know about Assessment*, Hodder and Stoughton, 1988
The Mathematical Association, *Maths Talk*, Stanley Thornes, 1987
Mitchell, C and V Koshy, *Effective Teacher Assessment*, Hodder and Stoughton, 1993

How to use this book ▷

This book has been tied to National Curriculum Attainment Targets so that the assessment tasks can be accessed easily. Within each of the sections – using and applying mathematics, number and algebra, and shape, space and measures – the tasks have been arranged by Level, with Level 1 exercises first, and so on. Our intention has been to provide a bank of short assessment tasks covering all Attainment Targets. However, we hope that readers will, rather than taking the book wholesale, choose and use those tasks which they find most useful, to support their own assessment judgements.

The copymasters (labelled 'A') are also marked to indicate to which AT and Level they refer. Reassessment copymasters are labelled 'B'. At the end of the book are two record sheets, enabling you to keep a class record and a record of the assessment tasks tried by each child.

Assessment across the Mathematics Curriculum

Children's learning in particular areas of mathematics should contribute to their understanding in others. Work can sometimes provide assessments for more than one Attainment Target. Here are examples showing mathematical settings for assessment in AT1 where assessments in AT2 or AT3 or both could also be made.

AT1, LEVEL 1

The children will probably not need direct intervention on your part to demonstrate that they can use mathematics in class activities. For example, they can be observed and assessed when:

- making junk models (also AT3)
- working out how many pencils, books etc to collect for their group (also AT2)

Children can show their thinking using the things around them and discussion by, for example:

- telling a classmate the steps in solving a problem like how many ears to give a row of seven policemen, using Lego® models or dolls (also AT2)
- showing the class their finished work and saying what they did when they made a birthday card by folding paper and drawing a numeral on it (also AT2 and AT3)

Pattern making and recognition can be demonstrated when, for example:

- walking around the school buildings and taking a good look (also AT3)
- using mosaic blocks, coloured paper or beads (also AT2 and AT3)

AT1, LEVEL 2

In order to give children independence of action in carrying through maths tasks, try letting them gather their own resources from the bank of resources in the classroom. They could then, for example:

- show that they choose a 30 cm ruler to measure a book, but a 1-metre stick to measure the classroom (also AT3)
- collect a variety of small things of different shapes and materials for sorting (also AT2)

Mathematical language both oral and written can be shown, when, for example, they:

- arrange models for a mathematical display (also AT3)
- make a little book on how much of which foods are consumed by a variety of pets, and read aloud from it (also AT2)

During discussion times you can offer children opportunities to make predictions like the following:

- four people went home to dinner last Friday and three on the Friday before that. It is Friday again today; how many do you think will go home today? What is likely to be the total number of people going home for dinner for all three Fridays? (also AT2)
- what usually happens after play (also AT2)
- what might happen if we put more cubes on this side of the balance? (also AT3)

AT1, LEVEL 3

To let children demonstrate that they can solve problems they can be given open-ended maths activities. Here are some examples from *Blueprints Maths Investigations*:

- design a badge or logo using symmetry (Investigation 40; also AT3)
- invent a shape trail (Investigation 42; also AT3)
- explore the Möbius strip (Investigation 27; also AT3)

You can see from their efforts how they organize what they are doing and whether they checked their work.

Children can discuss their thinking and their mathematics when reporting to the class about their work:

- how they solved a number problem involving pocket-money toys in the classroom shop (also AT2)
- how they recorded what they found out about the life cycle of a frog, moth or dragonfly (also AT3)

Look at a variety of ways of presenting findings, using symbols and diagrams, and let the children choose and adapt that which they think appropriate in a variety of situations. For example:

- survey data (also AT2)
- designing a contents plan for a maths resource cupboard (also AT2)

While investigating general statements like the following, children enhance their competence in number work:

- all even numbers are divisible by 2 (also AT2)
- the product of any number multiplied by 9 will reduce to the digit 9 (also AT2)

Similarly, the assessment tasks in this book can be used flexibly. How a child tackles a task can provide assessment information for work in several areas of mathematics.

AT1: Using and Applying Mathematics

Level Description

LEVEL 1

Pupils use mathematics as an integral part of classroom activities. They represent their work with objects or pictures and discuss it. They recognise and use a simple pattern or relationship, usually based on their experience.

TASK 1 — MATHS IN PRACTICAL TASKS A/B
C1-2

Resources
Classroom equipment including pencils, rubbers, paper and rulers, chalks and crayons, modelling materials, PE kit, overall and art materials, resource storage, books, play shop, beads, percussion instrument, junk model materials, dressing-up box, construction toys, jugs, buckets and other containers.

Organization
The children can work in groups to carry out the work for these assessments though you need to establish that each individual completes all tasks on the copymaster.

What you do
Over a period of time which may be days, weeks, or months give each child the opportunity to demonstrate that they use maths in the situations listed on C1.

Tick those demonstrated.

What the child does
Over a period of days, weeks or months, during the course of each school day, the child is given the opportunity to use maths in all the settings on C1.

Key question
Does the child use maths ideas and concepts in all they do around the classroom?

Reassessment
Use copymaster C2 (maths in practical tasks B) to carry out the reassessment.

Resources for reassessment are as follows: books, board game and counters, classroom equipment including crayons, paper, pencils, rulers, felt-tips, construction toys, display, play house or hospital, blocks, modelling materials, containers.

TASK 2 — TALK/ANSWER QUESTIONS ABOUT OBJECTS A/B
C3-4

Resources
Construction kit with parts that fit together, for example, Lasy®, Lego®; play farm animals or wild animals.

Organization
The child must work alone in the two tasks of creating a model and a layout of animals but can do it among other children, and can talk about it in front of other children providing that this gives no advantage to children who have still to do the task.

What you do
Review with the child the work done, once the model is complete. Ask them to tell you about the model, how they made it, why they made it as they did and any problems they had. Record in summary on C3 what is said.

For the animal layout you may like to offer a location, for example, a 'cushion mountain', or a 'rock island' in a bowl of water. Discuss the animal layout when that is done. Invite the child to move animals while telling a little story about them.

Encourage the child to use mathematical words. Take part so that the child can answer questions like, 'How many hippos would be left if one escaped?' and 'If we put the rabbits and guinea pigs in the same pen how many animals would then be living in the pen?'

What the child does
The child does two tasks in separate sessions.

The first task for the child is to make a model of their choice from a construction kit, and then talk to the teacher about it.

The second task for the child is to make a play farm or wild animal park layout and then talk to the teacher about that, while telling a story about the animals and, with the teacher's encouragement, using mathematical words in the story.

Key question
Can the child talk and pose or answer questions about their work?

Reassessment
Use copymaster C4 (talk/answer questions about work with objects B). Offer the child a different kind of resource from which to make a model. Examples include plastic straws which link together, or Bauhaus®. For the layout give them access to play house resources for a meal time. These may include a table, tablecloth, chairs, crockery, cutlery, toys to sit at table, and play food.

TASK 3 — USING PATTERN A/B
C5-6

Resources
Coloured beads, counters or buttons and paper squares – including enough of each colour to create and continue a pattern – coloured pencils.

Organization
This work is done individually.

What you do
Lay out a short row of beads with a repeat pattern of colour. Invite the child to continue the pattern and then copy the pattern by colouring the outlines on copymaster C5. Ask them to create and colour in their own bead patterns.

What the child does
Following instructions, the child is required to recognize, continue and copy the pattern, and then invent and copy two more of their own.

Key question
Can the child recognize and use pattern?

Reassessment
Set out a short row of coloured-paper squares so that a repeat pattern is apparent. Give the child more squares and copymaster C6 (using pattern B). Proceed as for assessment, then let the child arrange and colour two more patterns.

LEVEL 2

Level Description

Pupils select the mathematics for some classroom activities. They discuss their work using familiar mathematical language and are beginning to represent it using symbols and simple diagrams. They ask and respond appropriately to questions including 'What would happen if...?'.

TASK 4 — CHOOSE TOOLS AND MATHS FOR A TASK A/B
C7-8

Resources
None.

Organization
The child works alone.

What you do
Give the child copymaster C7 and invite them to show which tools they would use for which job. Point out that more than one tool can be used for a job, and the tools can be used more than once. Discuss the outcomes to establish that the child understands the mathematics involved.

What the child does
The child responds to the task on copymaster C7, and talks about the decisions made.

Key question
Can the child make appropriate choices about tools and mathematics to use?

Reassessment
Use copymaster C8 (choose tools and mathematics for a task B).

TASK 5 — TALK ABOUT HOW TO DO A MATHS TASK A/B
C9-10

Resources
None.

Organization
To be done individually.

What you do
Show the child copymaster C9, and ask them to tell you how they would try to solve these problems. You may need to ask questions to establish that the child understands the maths involved.

What the child does
The child discusses how they might tackle the tasks on copymaster C9. For example, in the third picture, the child may say, 'I could put the shapes with four side together'.

Key question
Can the child choose the appropriate mathematics to solve problems?

Reassessment
Invite the child to discuss solutions to tasks on copymaster C10 (talk about how to do a mathematics task B).

TASK 6
C11
-14
USE MATHS LANGUAGE A/B AND PREFER/DISLIKE LIST A/B

Resources
Nine children to give the information about themselves.

Organization
The task of getting information can be given to a number of children, providing each one works on a different topic.

Each child can give a feedback talk to the teacher, a group or the whole class.

What you do
Photocopy copymaster C13 (preference list A) on to card and then give each child a strip with a pair of items on it. The children can ask their classmates, 'Which do you prefer?' For example: 'Do you prefer jam or honey?'

Observe how each child goes about the task and make a record on copymaster C11, both of what happened and of how they talked about their efforts.

What the child does
They are to record the replies to the question they ask of nine classmates, and their own answers to the questions. Then they can let you know how they tackled the task.

Key question
Can the child use maths language when talking about or asking about their work?

Reassessment
Choose another question for the child to ask classmates. There are suggested pairs of items on copymaster C14 (dislikes list B) . Follow the instructions as for C11 above and then direct the children to ask, 'Which do you like less?'

Check their capacity to use maths language and record in the appropriate place on copymaster C12.

TASK 7
C15
-16
MATHEMATICAL DIAGRAM: BLOCK GRAPH A/B

Resources
Access to other children, rough paper and squared paper.

Organization
Children do need to produce their own block graphs. The information collection phase can be done in twos or threes.

What you do
Give each child a copy of copymaster C15. Explain what needs to be done and arrange groupings. Allow the children access to squared paper. When they have completed their block graph ask them to interpret the one on copymaster C15. You may prefer them to do the interpretation task before constructing their own block graph.

What the child does
The child follows the instructions on copymaster C15 (with the guidance of the teacher) and collects information which is then set out in a block graph. The child then answers the questions regarding the block graph presented on copymaster C15.

Key question
Can the child construct and interpret block graphs as examples of mathematical diagrams?

Reassessment
Show the children copymaster C16 and give them the opportunity to collect the information and set it down in a block graph. Then ask them to make the interpretations necessary using the block graph on copymaster 16.

TASK 8
C17
-18
MAKE MATHEMATICAL PREDICTIONS A/B

Resources
None.

Organization
Each child needs to study the copymaster alone, and then talk individually to the teacher.

What you do
Give the child copymaster C17 and ask them to think about what will happen 'next' or 'soon'. When they have had time to think it over, talk about the predictions.

What the child does
The child needs to think about what is going to happen in each of the situations on the copymaster. They could draw in what happens. They then need to discuss possible outcomes with the teacher. Note that there are not set 'right' answers to these situations. Using mathematical understanding, predictions might include things like:

- the drink level will go down in the glass
- the jigsaw shapes, put in correctly, will complete the numeral '6'
- the sixth person will complete a one-two-three pyramid
- the pointer on the scales will move to show the elephant's mass, or the scales platform will go down
- only five cakes will be left in the tray
- the knitting will get longer and the ball will get smaller
- the next cake will have four candles
- two faces will be left over

Key question
Can the child make mathematical predictions?

Reassessment
Give the child copymaster C18 (make predictions B). Here example predictions include the following:

- the liquid will overflow the glass
- the dog will grow even bigger

- the two pieces placed appropriately will complete the jigsaw
- nothing will happen when the feather is put in the balance pan because...
- the die may fall with any number from one to six showing
- perhaps a bigger pair of shoes is needed
- one more fish makes three and the water level will rise
- the coin will go in the till in exchange for the ice-cream; it may be the right money or there may be some change

TASK 9 — RESPOND TO 'WHAT IF?' A/B
C19 -20

Resources
None.

Organization
This is done individually.

What you do
Help the child by reading aloud each challenge from copymaster C19, while they look on. Note if the child can understand and respond.

What the child does
The child looks on and reads while the teacher reads out the challenges on the copymaster. The child responds to each in turn.

Key question
Can the child respond to the sorts of questions that begin with 'What if...?'

Reassessment
Carry out the reassessment using copymaster C20 (respond to 'what if?' B).

LEVEL 3

Level Description

Pupils try different approaches and find ways of overcoming difficulties that arise when they are solving problems. They are beginning to organise their work and check results. Pupils discuss their mathematical work and are beginning to explain their thinking. They use and interpret mathematical symbols and diagrams. Pupils show that they understand a general statement by finding particular examples that match it.

TASK 10 — OVERCOME PROBLEM-SOLVING DIFFICULTIES A/B
C21 -22

Resources
Rough paper, graph paper, classmates and possibly the register or school data base.

Organization
The child needs to work alone but must get information from nine classmates first.

What you do
Give copymaster C21, rough paper and graph paper to the child and talk through the task so that they can identify the difficulties encountered.

What the child does
The child has to follow the instructions on copymaster C21.

Key question
Is the child attempting to solve problems using appropriate mathematical strategies?

Reassessment
Use copymaster C22 (overcome problem solving difficulties B), and similar resources to those used for assessment A.

TASK 11 — ORGANIZING AND CHECKING RESULTS A/B
C23 -24

Resources
Nine other children to give information, and rough paper and a ruler.

Organization
The setting down of results is an individual effort.

What you do
Copymaster C23 offers six suggested information lists, linked to birthdays. You can give each child one of the lists. Ask each child to ask nine other children to answer a question related to the list. They should then add their own answers to the question posed, and present the findings, having checked that they have mustered and accurately recorded their results. They could, for example, find out each child's three favourites by asking:

- which three party foods do you like to eat most?
- which are the three best games to play at a birthday party?
- if you were taken out for a birthday treat which three places would you like to go?
- which three things would you most like to find in a party bag?

Examine the child's presentation of the results.

What the child does
The child collects information in rough, and collates and checks the results to make a presentation.

Key question
Can the child organize results clearly: are they comprehensive and easy to understand?

Reassessment
Offer the child one of the information lists from copymaster C24 (written presentation of results B) and let him present the results of this enquiry.

TASK 12 EXPLAINING MATHEMATICAL THINKING A/B
C25 -26

Resources
A set of dominoes, rough paper.

Organization
This investigative work has to be done individually.

What you do
Give the child the set of dominoes and some rough paper. Ask them to find out all they can about the number patterns on the dominoes.

They may, for example, choose to look at how many ones, twos etc there are, or the total numbers of dots on each domino, but they can decide this. Ask them to make rough notes and then make a written presentation of what they found on copymaster C25. They can then explain their thinking to you.

What the child does
The child examines the dominoes, finds patterns and using rough notes completes a fair presentation which they explain to the teacher.

Key question
Is the child able to explain clearly their mathematical thinking?

Reassessment
Using two dice ask the child to investigate the possible number patterns obtained when they are thrown. Then, using their rough notes, they write a fair copy on copymaster C26 (explaining mathematical thinking B).

TASK 13 USING MATHEMATICAL WORDS A/B
C27 -28

Resources
None.

Organization
An individual record on copymaster C27 can be kept by the teacher or child.

What you do
Over a period of days or weeks, keep a record of the mathematical words the child uses incidentally in classroom activities. Those on copymaster C27 are merely representative and come from the National Curriculum Statutory Orders (Levels 1–3). Additional or alternative words can be written alongside those listed.

What the child does
If you wish, the child can keep a copy of the 'word record' and tick the words they understand and use or they can compile their own 'maths words' books.

Key question
Can the child understand and use mathematical words?

Reassessment
Use C28 (using mathematical words B). Here the format is different, allowing the child to make a concertina book. You can use this to add to portfolios, for the child to check off words that you have indicated they know, and as a word list from which to devise maths games like 'What am I?' where one child has to explain the meaning of a word while another child tries to guess what the word is.

TASK 14 INTERPRET/CONSTRUCT PICTOGRAMS A/B
C29 -30

Resources
Access to the numbers of children who have school dinners one selected day in the week.

Organization
Information collection as required for copymaster C29 can be done in pairs or threes. Chart compilation should be done individually, as should the interpretation of the chart on copymaster C29.

What you do
Give the children a copy of copymaster C29 and ensure that they understand the task. Give them the time to collect and present their information. In another session allow the children to complete the interpretation part of copymaster C29.

What the child does
The child is asked to collect the information requested on C29 and to make a pictogram from the information. They also have to interpret the pictogram relating to 'clapometer' readings for magic acts.

Key question
Can the child construct and interpret pictograms as examples of mathematical diagrams?

Reassessment
Use copymaster C30 (interpret/construct mathematical diagrams : pictogram B). For this the children will need information about the number of right-handed people in each class.

TASK 15

C31 -32

FIND OUT BY TRYING EXAMPLES A/B

Resources
Scissors, squared paper.

Organization
Each child works individually.

What you do
Tell the children that a number of differently shaped patterns can be made with squares and that the number of possible shapes increases with the number of squares used. These are called polyominoes. Invite them to test this out, using the squares provided on copymaster C31.

What the child does
The child cuts out some squares from the paper and lays them down so that at least one edge of each square touches an edge of at least one other square, using firstly two squares, then three and so on. Alternatively, the child can draw on or colour in the copymaster to show patterns of two squares, then three squares and so on.

Key question
Can the child confirm the general statement by reference to their own trials?

Reassessment
Give the child triangular dotty paper on copymaster C32 (find out by trying examples B), and invite them to investigate the patterns to be made with numbers of triangles.

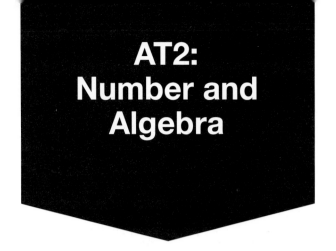

AT2:
Number and
Algebra

Level Description

Pupils count, order, add and subtract numbers when solving problems involving up to 10 objects. They read and write the numbers involved. Pupils recognise and make repeating patterns, counting the number of each object in each repeat.

TASK 1
C33-34

COUNT, RECOGNIZE, TALK ABOUT NUMBERS A/B

Resources
None.

Organization
Each child needs to have individual attention from the teacher to do this assessment task.

What you do
Place C33 in front of the child and let them count while you look on. They then point to and read out the numerals in order. Talk about the groups of creatures at the bottom of the page. The dividers across the groups give the child the opportunity to compare numbers of objects in pictures and say where there are more, fewer, and the same number. The word list at the bottom includes some of the key words the child should understand and use though they may not be able to read them all yet.

What the child does
The child works through C33 with the teacher.

Key question
Can the child count, recognize numerals and talk about numbers?

Reassessment
Carry through the tasks as above using copymaster C34 (count, recognize and talk about numbers B).

Organization
This must be done individually.

What you do
Cut out the number word flash cards from the bottom of the copymaster C35. Using pencils, marbles and blocks, offer the child a number of items, firstly up to five, then up to ten, and watch them count the items. Do this offering counts from one to five and then one to ten in any order. Tick on copymaster C35 if this is achieved.

Then ask the child to write the numbers one to ten on a rough piece of paper (while you check off the corresponding numerals on the copymaster).

Finally ask them to read out the number words from the flash cards as you present them. Try presenting them several times, changing the order on each occasion. This set of cards can then be for the child's individual use, if the work needs reinforcement before a re-test.

What the child does
Under the direction of the teacher the child counts objects, writes numerals and reads words for numbers.

Key question
Can the child count to ten, write numerals up to ten and read the number words from one to ten?

Reassessment
Using copymaster C36, crayons, small balls and counting apparatus, let the child do counts like those suggested in assessment above. Then ask the child to write numerals and point to and read number words as in the assessment task.

TASK 2
C35-36

COUNT, READ AND WRITE NUMBERS A/B

Resources
Pencils, marbles, blocks, and paper.

TASK 3
C37-38

ADD AND SUBTRACT USING A FEW OBJECTS A/B

Resources
Shells, conkers, books, marbles and small toys.

Organization

The child being assessed can work as part of a group, but must have plenty of opportunities to demonstrate their own knowledge.

What you do

Present the child with a small number of objects either while they are in a group or when they are on their own. During a number of sessions ask them to put small groups of objects together and find the totals, and talk about what they are doing. In a subsequent series of sessions ask them to take away items from a pile of objects and talk about what they are doing and what is left. Record the totals to which they can add and from which they can take away on C37.

What the child does

Following the teacher's directions, the child is required to demonstrate that they can add groups of classroom objects and subtract items from a group of objects using numbers from one to ten.

Key question

Can the child add and subtract numbers of objects to ten?

Reassessment

Follow the strategy as above using C38 (add and subtract using a small number of objects B) and the following resources: counting apparatus, crayons, paint brushes and fruit.

TASK 4 — REPEATING PATTERNS A/B

C39-40

Resources

None.

Organization

This task is done individually.

What you do

Give the child copymaster C39 to complete, and explain what to do.

What the child does

The child continues the patterns on copymaster C39 and then invents and draws some of their own.

Key question

Can the child recognize, replicate and invent repeat patterns?

Reassessment

Allow the child to work alone on copymaster C40 (repeating patterns B).

LEVEL 2

Level Description

Pupils count sets of objects reliably, and use mental recall of addition and subtraction facts to 10. They have begun to understand the place value of each digit in a number and use this to order numbers up to 100. They choose the appropriate operation when solving addition and subtraction problems. They identify and use halves and quarters, such as half of a rectangle or a quarter of eight objects. They recognise sequences of numbers, including odd and even numbers.

TASK 5 — PATTERNS IN ADDITION/ SUBTRACTION TO 10 A/B

C41-42

Resources

Counting aids or apparatus, and rough paper.

Organization

The children need to work independently on these tasks.

What you do

Give the children copymaster C41 to complete and check that they understand what is required of them.

What the child does

The child completes work on copymaster C41 using counting aids if necessary.

Key question

Can the child demonstrate that they can identify patterns in addition and subtraction?

Reassessment

Give the child copymaster C42 (patterns in addition and subtraction B) to complete.

TASK 6 — ADDITION/ SUBTRACTION FACTS TO 10 A/B

C43-44

Resources

None are essential. Counting aids can be used to demonstrate place value.

Organization

This work is done individually.

What you do

Give the child copymaster C43 to complete.

What the child does

Fill in the missing numbers on copymasters C43. This task could be combined with others at Level 2.

Key question
Does the child know the number patterns in addition and subtraction to ten?

Reassessment
Give the child copymaster C44 (addition and subtraction facts to 10 B) and ask them to complete the tasks as above.

TASK 7 — NUMBERS TO 100 AND PLACE VALUE A/B
C45 -46

Resources
Counting aids.

Organization
This is individual work.

What you do
Give the child copymaster C45 and ask them to complete it.

What the child does
The child completes copymaster C45 using counting aids as necessary.

Key question
Can the child demonstrate an understanding of place value?

Reassessment
Give the child copymaster C46 (numbers to 100 and place value B) to complete.

TASK 8 — FIND THE DIFFERENCE PROBLEMS A/B
C47 -48

Resources
Crayons, books and shoe bags, small items set out in a class shop. These could be play dough cakes, or little clay models.

Find the difference problems which can be set among classroom displays or drawn on large sheets of paper and displayed about the room.

Organization
This assessment involves a variety of activities. The problems involving class equipment and stories and finding the difference can be done alone. Shop play involves other children.

What you do
Set the child the following sets of problems:

- addition and subtraction problems involving crayons, books and shoebags
- two number stories with problems in them involving beans and bears. Use as starting points Jack and the Beanstalk and The Three Bears but invent changes

to the numbers in the stories and the story-lines so that addition and subtraction problems arise for the children to solve. For example: if five magic beans from ten were lost how many were left? If only three beans made wishes come true how many beans were not wish beans?

- shopping problems set in the class shop
- challenges to 'find the difference' between numbers of items set out in any classroom displays or drawn on a large sheet of paper

Record on copymaster C47 the outcomes of the child's efforts.

What the child does
Tackles the problems as set.

Key question
Can the child do addition and subtraction problems?

Reassessment
Follow the procedure as above using copymaster C48 (find the difference problems B) and resources that include rulers, erasers and boxes and class shop items which may include greeting cards, stamps, or gift tags. The number problem stories involve using as starting points the stories The Runaway Pancake and The Three Little Pigs and inventing new versions as shown in the assessment version above. Example questions here might include the following:

- if five animals chased the pancake and two fell down how many would still be in the chase?
- if the bears had Grandma and Grandad to stay how many porridge bowls would be needed?

TASK 9 — MISSING NUMBER PROBLEMS A/B
C49 -50

Resources
None.

Organization
Children need to work alone for this assessment. It could be given to a group or class, provided the children are unable to see one another's work.

What you do
Give the children copymaster C49 to complete. Work out an answer sheet.

What the child does
The child works on copymaster C49.

Key question
Can the child understand and solve 'missing number' problems?

Reassessment
Give the child copymaster C50 (missing numbers B) to complete.

TASK 10 — HALVES AND QUARTERS A/B

C51
-52

Resources
None.

Organization
Each child works individually.

What you do
Give each child copymaster C51 and ask them to complete it.

What the child does
The child works on copymaster C51.

Key question
Does the child recognize a half and a quarter?

Reassessment
Use copymaster C52 (halves and quarters B).

TASK 11 — ODDS AND EVENS A/B

C53
-54

Resources
Counting aids or apparatus, and rough paper.

Organization
The children need to work independently on this task.

What you do
Ask the children to work on copymaster C53.

What the child does
The child completes copymaster C53.

Key question
Can the child demonstrate an understanding of odd and even numbers?

Reassessment
Give the child C54 (odds and evens B) to complete.

LEVEL 3 — Level Description

Pupils show understanding of place value in numbers up to 1000 and use this to make approximations. They have begun to use decimal notation and to recognise negative numbers in contexts such as money, temperature, and calculator displays. Pupils use mental recall of addition and subtraction facts to 20 in solving problems involving larger numbers. They use mental recall of the 2, 5 and 10 multiplication tables, and others up to 5 x 5, in solving whole-number problems involving multiplication or division, including those that give rise to remainders. Pupils use calculator methods where numbers include several digits. They have begun to develop mental strategies and use them to find methods for adding and subtracting numbers with at least two digits.

TASK 12 — INTERPRETING BIG NUMBERS A/B

C55
-56

Resources
None are essential.

Organization
This assessment is done independently by each child.

What you do
Give the child copymaster C55 to complete.

What the child does
The child is required to fill in numbers on the copymaster.

Key question
Does the child know about place value in numbers to 1,000?

Reassessment
Give the child copymaster C56 (interpreting big numbers B) to complete as above.

TASK 13 — APPROXIMATION A/B

C57
-58

Resources
None.

Organization
This must be done individually.

What you do
Give the child copymaster C57 to complete.

What the child does
The child fills in approximations on copymaster C57.

Key question
Can the child make approximations?

Reassessment
Give the child copymaster C58 (approximation) to complete.

TASK 14 — C59 -60 — DECIMAL MONEY A/B

Resources
None.

Organization
The children are required to work individually on this task.

What you do
Give the child copymaster C59.

What the child does
The child completes the shopping challenges on the copymaster. You may let the children check the work of others using calculators.

Key question
Can the child work with decimal money?

Reassessment
Give the child copymaster C60 (decimal money B) to complete.

TASK 15 — C61 -62 — NEGATIVE NUMBERS A/B

Resources
Reference books about cold places on earth, a calculator.

Organization
The worksheet must be done independently.

What you do
Give the child copymaster C61 to complete. Let them show you their calculator work.

What the child does
The child completes copymaster C61.

Key question
Does the child demonstrate an understanding of negative numbers in the context of temperature?

Reassessment
Give the child copymaster C62 to complete (negative numbers B). Show them a maximum and minimum thermometer so that they can observe and draw the scale.

TASK 16 — C63 -64 — ADD AND SUBTRACT TO 20 INCLUDING 0 A/B

Resources
None.

Organization
This is to be done individually.

What you do
Give the child copymaster C63 to complete. Observe the child at work. The work should involve mental skills. If a child is laboriously wading through this sheet, and working without using memory or a knowledge of patterns, there may be a case for a reworking of the opportunity to commit number bonds to memory.

What the child does
The child completes copymaster C63.

Key question
Can the child add and subtract up to 20, including 0, with ease?

Reassessment
Give the child copymaster C64 (add and subtract to 20 including 0) and observe them at work.

TASK 17 — C65 -66 — 2, 5, 10 X TABLES AND UP TO 5 X 5 A/B

Resources
None.

Organization
The children complete this on their own.

What you do
Give the child copymaster C65 and ask them to write down the 2, 5 and 10 x tables and complete the little problems at the bottom.

What the child does
The child completes copymaster C65. The space provided allows for 1 x through to 10 x.

Key question
Does the child know their two, five and ten times tables and all multiples up to five times five?

Reassessment
Give the child copymaster C66 (2, 5, 10 x tables and up to 5 x 5 B) and similar instructions to those above.

TASK 18 — C67 -68 — DIVISION BY 2, 5 AND 10 A/B

Resources
Coloured pencils.

Organization
This work is done individually.

What you do
Give the children copymaster C67 to complete. The children should colour one or more of each set of lights.

What the child does
The child completes copymaster C67.

Key question
Does the child know of numbers divisible by two, five or ten?

Reassessment
Give the child copymaster C67 (division by 2, 5 or 10 B) to complete by colouring in the appropriate leaves.

TASK 19 MULTIPLICATION AND DIVISION PROBLEMS A/B
C69 -70

Resources
None.

Organization
This is done individually by the child, independent of the teacher.

What you do
Give the child copymaster C69. Work out the answers ready for marking.

What the child does
The child completes copymaster C69.

Key question
Has the child shown that they can do multiplication and division problems?

Reassessment
Give the child copymaster C70 (multiplication and division problems B) to complete.

TASK 20 REMAINDERS A/B
C71 -72

Resources
Counting aids if required.

Organization
Children can do this independently of one another, but you can then ask them to check and mark one another's work.

What you do
Prepare an answer sheet. Ask each child to complete copymaster C71.

What the child does
The child can complete work on copymaster C71 and then check and mark the work of a classmate.

Key question
Can the child cope with remainders?

Reassessment
Give the child copymaster C72 (remainders B) to complete and proceed as for the assessment.

TASK 21 USING A CALCULATOR A/B
C73 -74

Resources
A calculator for each child.

Organization
Children work alone on the calculations. If each child checks the work of another child this will give additional evidence of their calculator competence

What you do
Invite the child to work out the calculations on copymaster C73 using the calculator. Ask them to discuss any difficulties with you as they go along, for you need this evidence in addition to the completed task sheet in order to make an assessment.

What the child does
The child completes the calculations on copymaster C73 using a calculator. They can then check the answers gained by another child, again using the calculator.

Key question
Is the child competent in using a calculator?

Reassessment
Give the child copymaster C74 (using a calculator B) to work on, and then let them check the work of another child.

TASK 22 MENTAL COMPUTATION STRATEGIES A/B
C75 -76

Resources
None.

Organization
This is done individually.

What you do
Give the child copymaster C75 to complete. If you have time, the patterns and calculations could be talked through with children individually. Some children may, for example, find it difficult to describe on paper how they do the calculations at the bottom of copymaster C75 but may be able to explain very well orally.

What the child does
The child completes copymaster C75, discussing with the teacher their strategies.

Key question

Can the child detect and use patterns and other mental strategies when doing computation and explain the methods used?

Reassessment

Ask the child to complete copymaster C76 (mental computation strategies B), and discuss with you the strategies they used.

Resources

None.

Organization

Can be done among other children, by individuals.

What you do

Give the child copymaster C77 to complete. Work out an answer sheet. This is exemplar material. If Lego® is available the children should have experience of this too.

What the child does

The child completes copymaster C77.

Key question

Has the child the mental strategies to deal with function machines?

Reassessment

Give the child copymaster C78 (function machines B) to complete.

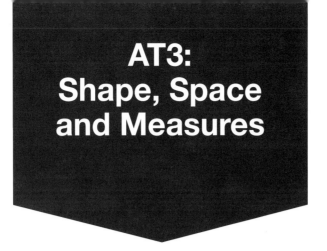

AT3: Shape, Space and Measures

LEVEL 1

Level Description

When working with 3-D and 2-D shapes, pupils use everyday language to describe properties and positions. They measure and order objects using direct comparison, and order events.

TASK 1

SHAPE TALK A/B

C79 -80

Resources
A wide variety of 3-D and 2-D shapes including everyday shapes like those found in packaging and mathematical apparatus and plastic and card 2-D shapes; not all the shapes need to be regular but cubes, cuboids, cylinders, spheres, squares, rectangles, circles, triangles, hexagons and pentagons need to be present. Lego® or similar apparatus.

Organization
Children need to work alone but can do so among other children.

What you do
Observe the child while they sort shapes and talk about them. Record the kinds of language used in describing the shapes and the sorting on copymaster C79. Discuss with the child the making of a Lego® or other model, recording some of the words the child uses.

What the child does
The child sorts 3-D and 2-D shapes a number of times and talks about what they are doing. They then make a model and talk about that to the teacher. Ideally the work should be done over a number of sessions. However, this puts heavy demands on the teacher's time. Note that the child is not required to 'name' shapes but should be able to identify similarities and differences between shapes, using everyday language.

Key question
Can the child use appropriate words when talking about shapes?

Reassessment
Use copymaster C80 (shape talk B). Proceed as above. Resources required include straws that link together and Plasticine®.

TASK 2

POSITION WORDS A/B

C81 -82

Resources
None.

Organization
The child works alone with the teacher on this assessment.

What you do
Place the copymaster before each child and listen while they show their ability to use words which describe position, when looking at copymaster C81. This should not take more than a few minutes.

What the child does
The child responds to the pictures on copymaster C81 by giving the position of the shoe.

Key question
Can the child use appropriate words when talking about position?

Reassessment
Ask the child to describe the positions of the beetle on copymaster C82 (position words B).

TASK 3

COMPARE AND ORDER OBJECTS AND EVENTS A/B

C83 -84

Resources
A number of pencils of different lengths, names or pictures of three children in the class, a variety of food packs of different sizes, pictures of children doing things they do before school (for example: get up, clean teeth, pack school bag, get dressed, eat breakfast).

Organization

Depending on the space and resources available, several children could work at this, selecting their own resources from a 'bank', or the resources can be set on display and the children can take turns to work with them.

What you do

Allow the child access to the resources listed. Ask the child to draw the things in order and then tell you about what they have drawn.

What the child does

The child places the things in each resource group in order and draws them on copymaster C83. Thus they draw the following:

- pencils in order of length
- friends in order of height
- food packs in order of size
- 'things I do' in time sequence

Key question

Can the child order things and events?

Reassessment

Offer the child the opportunity to do a similar exercise to the one above, using copymaster C84 (compare and order objects and events B). Provide the following resources: crayons, a view of a variety of buildings (from the window if possible), a variety of snacks of different sizes, a sequence of pictures showing a child changing into PE kit, playing a game and changing again afterwards. They are required to draw the following on the copymaster:

- crayons in order of length
- buildings in order of height
- snacks in order of size (or how heavy they feel in the hand)
- 'things I do' in time sequence

LEVEL 2

Level Description

Pupils use mathematical names for common 3-D and 2-D shapes and describe their properties, including numbers of sides and corners. They distinguish between straight and turning movements, understand angle as a measurement of turn, and recognise right angles in turns. They have begun to use everyday non-standard and standard units to measure length and mass.

TASK 4 — COMMON 2-D AND 3-D SHAPES A/B

C85 -86

Resources
None.

Organization
This work is done independently by each child.

What you do
Give the child copymaster C85 to complete.

What the child does
The child has to complete copymaster C85.

Key question
Can the child recognize common 2-D and 3-D shapes?

Reassessment
Offer the child copymaster C86 (common 2-D and 3-D shapes B) to work on.

TASK 5 — TYPES OF MOVEMENT A/B

C87 -88

Resources
The hall or other space to conduct a series of movement lessons.

Organization
To assess types of movement, conduct a series of movement classes with the whole class.

What you do
Conduct a series of movement classes as described on copymaster C87. Aim to observe and make judgements about half the children in the class through this means. The reassessment lessons can then be run for absentees and the remaining children in the class. If you wish, one sequence can extend to more than four lessons.

What the child does
The child is required to respond to a variety of challenges in a set of movement lessons.

Key question
Can the child recognize movements and angles?

Reassessment
Reassess (or assess those children who have not been observed) on types of movement by conducting the set of lessons as set out on copymaster C88 (types of movement B).

TASK 6 — RIGHT ANGLES A/B

C89 -90

Resources
None.

Organization
This work is done independently by each child.

What you do
Give the child copymaster C89 to complete.

What the child does
The child has to complete copymaster C89.

Key question
Can the child recognize right angles?

Reassessment
Offer the child copymaster C90 (right angles B) to work on.

What the child does
The children measure a variety of things using non-standard measures and using copymaster C91 write in and match the things they measured to the units or tools they used.

Key question
Can the child measure length and mass using non-standard units?

Reassessment
Give the child similar opportunities to those above, using copymaster C92 (non-standard measures: length and mass B).

TASK 7 — NON-STANDARD MEASURES: LENGTH AND MASS A/B
C91 -92

TASK 8 — STANDARD MEASURES: LENGTH AND MASS A/B
C93 -94

Resources
The children will require access to a variety of things in and around the classroom, from which they can take measurements. These could include furniture, aspects of the room itself, like the doorway or stationery and other classroom equipment. Children's own belongings including lunch boxes and pumps can be useful too.

Organization
The children can do the non-standard measuring in pairs, for it is the experience that is being assessed and not the accuracy of measurement.
  The record sheet of measures, C91, has to be done individually.

What you do
Organize the classroom and the timetable so that, over a period of time, the children have experience of measuring a variety of things using the non-standard measures listed on copymaster C91.

Resources
None.

Organization
This is done individually.

What you do
Give the child copymaster C93 to complete.

What the child does
The child has to write on copymaster C93 whether each measure is one of length or mass and match the units up to something the units may be used to measure.

Key question
Can the children demonstrate that they recognize common standard units for measuring length and mass?

Reassessment
Give the child copymaster C94 to complete.

LEVEL 3 — Level Description
Pupils classify 3-D and 2-D shapes in various ways using mathematical properties such as reflective symmetry. They use non-standard units and standard metric units of length, capacity, mass and time, in a range of contexts.

TASK 9 — SORTING SHAPES A/B
C95 -96

Resources
A large selection of cardboard shapes including irregular polygons, squares, rectangles, circles, triangles, hexagons and pentagons. These could be homemade or bought in but do include irregular as well as regular shapes. Add to this a collection of empty packaging including cubes, cuboids and cylinders.

Organization
Children need to have turns at this activity but it can be done as part of group work.

What you do
Observe while the children sort 2-D and 3-D shapes. Listen to their explanations for their sorts, and to their responses to the sorts done by others and record responses on copymaster C95.

What the child does
The children sort a variety of shapes, explain how they

did the sorting, and respond to the sorts done by other children.

Key question
Can the child sort shapes mathematically?

Reassessment
Use copy master C96 (sorting shapes B) to record how well the child works using mathematically accurate 3-D shapes and 2-D shape templates.

TASK
10
C97
-98

REFLECTIVE SYMMETRY A/B

Resources
None.

Organization
This activity is to be done independently by each child, but it can be given as a class 'test'.

What you do
Give each child a copy of copymaster C97 and explain that shapes showing reflective symmetry should be ringed, and that some lines and planes of symmetry should be drawn in.

What the child does
The child completes copymaster C97.

Key question
Can the child recognize reflective symmetry?

Reassessment
Use copymaster C98 (reflective symmetry B).

TASK
11
C99
-100

LENGTH, CAPACITY, MASS, TIME (NON-STANDARD UNITS) A/B

Resources
The children will require access to a variety of things in and around the classroom, from which they can take measurements.

Organization
The children can do the non-standard measuring in pairs,

for it is the experience that is being assessed and not the accuracy of measurement. The record sheet, C99, has to be completed individually.

What you do
Organize the classroom and the timetable so that, over a period of time, the children have experience of measuring a variety of things using the non-standard measures listed on copymaster C99.

What the child does
The child measures a variety of things using non-standard measures and using copymaster C99 they draw and write in the things they measured and match them to the measures they used.

Key question
Can the child make measurements using non-standard units?

Reassessment
Give the child copymaster C100 on which to record what they measured with which units.

TASK
12
C101
-102

LENGTH, CAPACITY, MASS, TIME (STANDARD UNITS) A/B

Resources
Coloured pencils in ten colours.

Organization
This is done individually.

What you do
Give the child copymaster C101 to complete, and a set of ten coloured pencils.

What the child does
The child has to join measurements with items on copymaster C101 to which the measurements may apply.

Key question
Can the children demonstrate that they recognize metric units for measuring and do they know how we measure time?

Reassessment
Give the child copymaster C102 to complete.

Name: _____ Date: _____

| A | Maths in practical tasks

Accesses enough equipment

Collects correct number of pencils for a group .... ❑

Checks seating is enough for a group .... ❑

Fetches enough modelling material to make desired model .... ❑

Collects one of each of a variety of items to do a task (for example: pencil,
    rubber, paper and ruler) .... ❑

Follows instructions to carry through a job

Fetches shoebag/undresses/puts on PE kit/leaves clothes tidy .... ❑

Collects modelling material/apron/works on model to completion/shows
    the teacher.. ❑

When instructed to write and then draw, does so .... ❑

Puts on overall, does a painting/shows the teacher .... ❑

Puts equipment away

Sorts pencils, chalks and crayons .... ❑

Sorts counting aids into labelled containers... ❑

Tidies books by section and size .... ❑

Tidies play shop placing items in order, cash in till, closed sign on door .... ❑

Makes patterns

Threads beads to own repeat pattern.. ❑

Invents a pattern of claps or beats with hands or percussion instrument .... ❑

Colours in a pattern using repeat colours... ❑

Invents a dance or movement sequence that can be repeated .... ❑

Builds models

Makes a junk model .... ❑

Makes a model on wheels .... ❑

Makes a clay or Plasticine® animal .... ❑

Makes a paper picture with 3-D elements .... ❑

Shows understanding of measurement

Uses size comparisons .... ❑

When dressing up uses ideas about size and fit .... ❑

In making models, makes 'roof' fit, chooses toy figures that match in scale .... ❑

Begins to choose containers suitable in size for proposed contents .... ❑

Name: _____ Date: _____

B | Maths in practical tasks

Accesses enough equipment
Collects correct number of books for a group .... ❏
Checks enough work space for a group .... ❏
Fetches enough counters to play a game with friends .... ❏
Collects one of each of a variety of items to do a task (for example: red crayon,
    blue crayon, piece of paper, pencil) .... ❏

Follows instructions to carry through a job
Gets ready to go home in specified order (for example, gets coat on, packs bag,
    puts chair up, lines up) .... ❏
Collects construction-toy box, makes a model, shows the teacher .... ❏
Takes a message to another part of school, brings back a reply .... ❏

Puts equipment away
Sorts rulers, felt-tips, coloured pencils .... ❏
Sorts counting aids into labelled containers .... ❏
Tidies a display, matching items to appropriate part of what is on show .... ❏
Tidies house or hospital putting all 'in order' for the next game .... ❏

Makes patterns
Sets out blocks in size, shape or colour pattern .... ❏
Makes up a pattern of sounds or words that repeat .... ❏
Uses repeat colours in a pattern on paper .... ❏
Invents an active game with a pattern of 'moves' that is repeated .... ❏

Builds models
Constructs a model house, tower or bridge .... ❏
Makes a clay or Plasticine® island .... ❏
Makes a mask .... ❏
Makes a model that helps to lift things (for example: a crane, a see-saw, a swing) .. ❏

Shows understanding of measurement
Uses size comparisons .... ❏
Makes models with parts that fit .... ❏
Chooses an appropriate container for milk, sand, polystyrene chippings .... ❏
Matches play bedclothes, tablecloths etc to appropriate furniture .... ❏

Name: _____ Date: _____

| A | Talk/answer questions about objects | C3 |

Model making
Materials used

_____

Describes model

_____

Explains how constructed

_____

Talks about choice of parts – shapes, sizes

_____

Discusses problems in making model

_____

• •

Play farm/safari park
Resources used

_____

Explains layout

_____

Moves items and tells a number story of events

_____

Responds to teacher action and questioning

_____

Name: _____ Date: _____

| B | Talk/answer questions about objects | C4 →

Model making
  Materials used

_____

Describes model

_____

Explains how constructed

_____

Talks about choice of parts – shapes, sizes

_____

Discusses problems in making model

_____

• •

Play mealtime
  Resources used

_____

Explains layout

_____

Tells a story using mealtime layout

_____

Responds to teacher action and questioning

_____

Name: _____ Date: _____

| A | Using pattern | C5 |

Colour to match

Colour your own patterns

Name: _____ Date: _____

B | Using pattern

Colour to match

Colour your own patterns

Name: _____ Date: _____

A | Choose tools and maths for a task

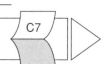

What would you use to find out these things?
You may need more than one

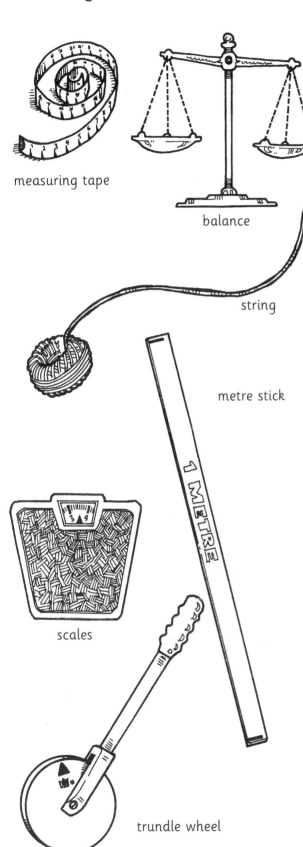

measuring tape

balance

string

metre stick

scales

trundle wheel

Which is heavier?

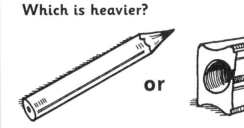

or

Tallest girl in class

Biggest table in school

Distance from school gate to school door

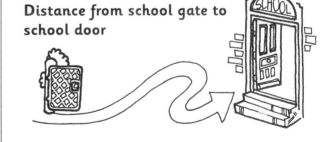

How heavy is the head teacher?

How long is a blade of grass?

Name: _____ Date: _____

B | Choose tools and maths for a task

What would you use to find out these things?

You may need more than one

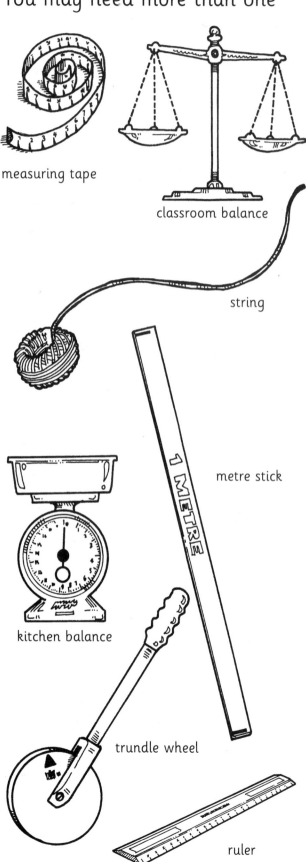

measuring tape

classroom balance

string

metre stick

kitchen balance

trundle wheel

ruler

Which is heavier? 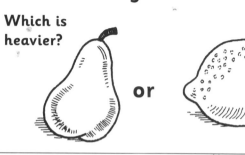 or

Shortest teacher

Biggest book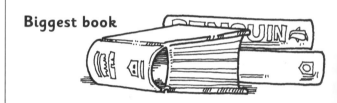

Length of a pencil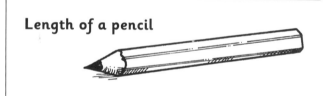

How much flour to make a cake?

Length of a running track

Name: _____ Date: _____

| A | Talk about how to do a maths task | |

Talk about how you work out these

The cost of two comics

How many apples
there will be?

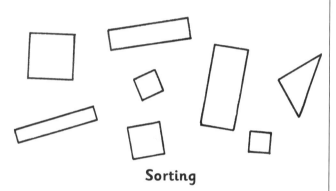

Sorting

The longest ball of wool

The biggest picture

How long until the holidays?

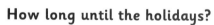

Which
holds more?

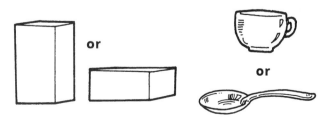

or

or

Which snack
is heaviest?

Name: _____ Date: _____

B | Talk about how to do a maths task

Talk about how you work out these

The cost of two toys

The biggest sticker

Sorting

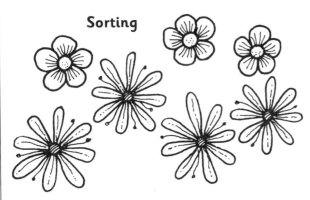

How long until home time?

Longest mop or broom

Which is heaviest?

How many cars would fill the car park?

Which holds more?

Name: ______________________ Date: __________

AT1 Level 2

A Use maths language

C11

Preference question given

Observation

Task completed .... ❑

Talk

Key sample words used

Name: _____ Date: _____

| B | Use maths language |

C12

Pet hate question given

Observation

Task completed .... ❑

Talk

Key sample words used

Name: _____ Date: _____

A | Preference list

Key question: which do you prefer?

ice cream   milkshake

apple   orange

cat   dog

ball games   play on a bike

carrot   tomato

jam   honey

milk   fruit juice

glove   mitten

hood   hat

biscuit   cake

Name: _____ Date: _____

| B | Dislikes list | C14 |

Key question: which do you like less?

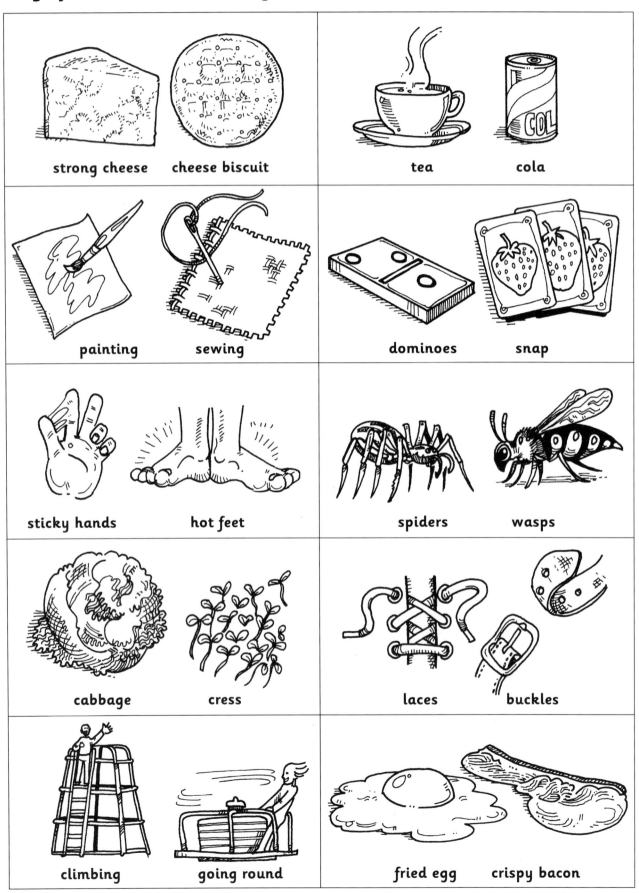

strong cheese	cheese biscuit	tea	cola
painting	sewing	dominoes	snap
sticky hands	hot feet	spiders	wasps
cabbage	cress	laces	buckles
climbing	going round	fried egg	crispy bacon

Name: _____ Date: _____

| A | Mathematical diagram: block graph | C15 |

Travel: block graph

- Names of 10 friends in school (including yourself)
- Ask each have you ever been on a   plane?
boat?
train?

- Write down what they say
- Draw a block graph

Where they live

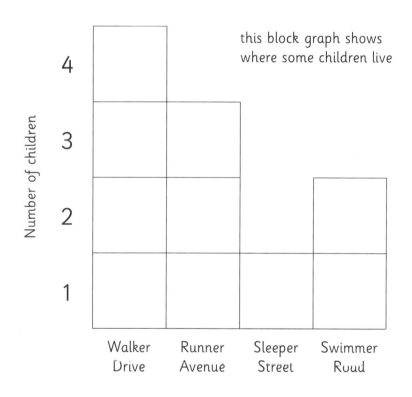

this block graph shows
where some children live

4 children live in _____

How many children altogether? [   ]

1 child lives in _____

Where do more children live: Runner Avenue or Swimmer Road?

_____

Name: _____ Date: _____

| B | Mathematical diagram: block graph | C16 |

Holidays: block graph

• Names of 10 friends in school (including yourself)
• Ask each one: have you ever had a holiday in a hotel?
cottage?
caravan?

• Write down what they say
• Draw a block graph

Out-of-school activities

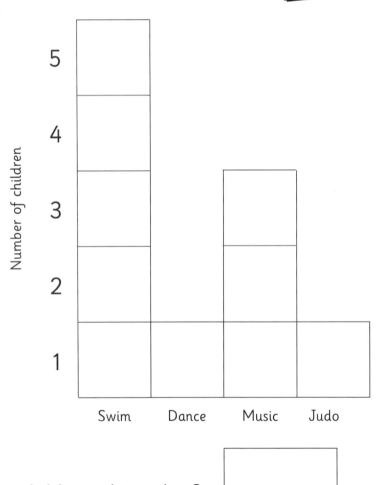

How many children altogether? ☐

_____ is the most popular activity

Do more children do music or dance? _____

How many children do judo? ☐

Name: _____ Date: _____

| A | Make mathematical predictions | C17 |

What do you think will happen next?

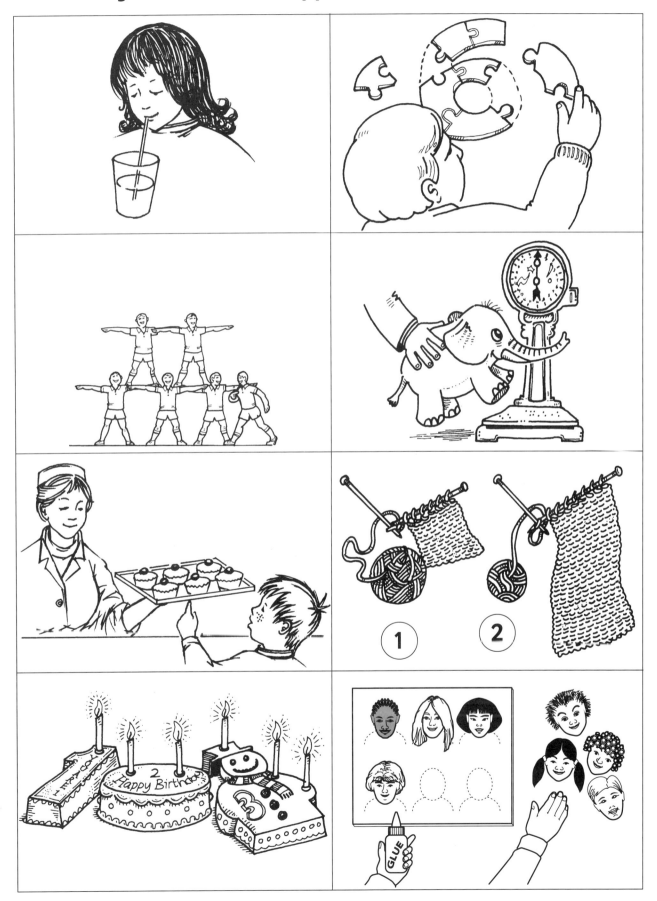

Name: _____ Date: _____

B │ Make mathematical predictions

What do you think will happen next?

A | Respond to 'What if?'

What happens to lesson time if playtime is made longer?

What happens if four shells weigh the same as six fir-cones and you add another fir-cone to the balance pan?

An ice-cream seller has vanilla, strawberry and chocolate ice-creams. What happens to sales of vanilla and strawberry when the chocolate ice-creams have all been sold?

What happens to a circle of children if they move from standing side by side to holding hands with arms outstretched?

What happens to the number of cakes you can make if you double the quantities of flour and eggs and other ingredients to make them?

Why does a game take longer if you have to throw a six on the die to start?

What happens to the level of bubble mixture as you use the mixture to blow bubbles?

If ten children wear cardigans on Thursday and twenty wear them on Friday, how do you think the weather report has changed?

If a string of beads has one red, one blue, one green, one red, one blue, one green on it, why does the next bead have to be red? What is the colour of the one after that?

Name: _____ Date: _____

| B | Respond to 'What if?' |

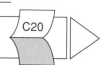

C20

What happens to a shoe-size graph as you and your friends get older?

If the shop selling pencil tops like crocodiles, bears and tigers sells out of bears, what happens to the sales of crocodiles and tigers?

If you have 12 pancakes with half a litre of milk in the batter, what happens to the number of pancakes if you make twice as much batter?

Why is it possible to build a taller tower with ten blocks than it is with five?

Out of five beanbags, Seb has thrown three in his bucket, and Deirdre four. Who is more likely to finish first?

What happens to the page numbers in a book as you turn on a page?

What happens to the number of the children in a class if four move house and go to another school?

What happens to a see-saw with one person on each end if another person gets on one end?

| A | Overcome problem-solving difficulties | C21 ▷ |

9 classmates

Write down their birthday months

Add your own birthday month

Draw a graph to show which months are birthday months

As you go along, tick any problems you have and write down how you solved them

How I solved it

Someone forgot their birthday month tick ☐	
I got in a muddle tick ☐	
My graph went wrong tick ☐	
Other problems (draw) tick ☐	

Name: _____ Date: _____

B │ Overcome problem-solving difficulties

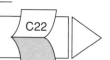

C22

Write down their shoe sizes

9 classmates
4 boys, 4 girls and
1 more girl (if you are a boy) or
1 more boy (if you are a girl)

Add your own shoe size

Draw a graph to show the number of children wearing each size

As you go along, tick any problems you have and write down how you solved them

How I solved it

I could not find out the shoe size tick ☐	
I got in a muddle tick ☐	
My graph went wrong tick ☐	
Other problems (draw) tick ☐	

Name: _____ Date: _____

A Organizing and checking results

C23

Party Foods

hamburger

pizza   cake

sausage   crisps

sandwich   jelly

cheese   ice cream

sausage roll

Party Games

blind man's buff
treasure hunt
statues
pass the parcel
Simon says
musical chairs

Fancy Dress

pirate
wild west
prince or princess
dancer
insect
monster
wild animal
police officer
doctor
mouse

Birthday Treats

swimming
cinema
hamburger restaurant
park
museum
zoo
seaside

Party Bag Gifts

balloon   paper hat

whistle   pencil

rubber   pencil sharpener

sticker   sweet bar

teddy   top

Birthday Card Pictures

cats
dogs
boys or girls
monsters
flowers
rabbits
rainbows
boats

Name: _____ Date: _____

B ‖ Organizing and checking results

Games

snakes and ladders
ludo
draughts
chess
tiddly-winks

Fairground Rides

dodgems
hook the duck
boat ride
coconut shy
shooting gallery
haunted house

Sports

football
swimming
snooker
tennis
athletics
show jumping

Playground Games

tick
hide-and-seek
skipping
hopscotch
marbles
ball

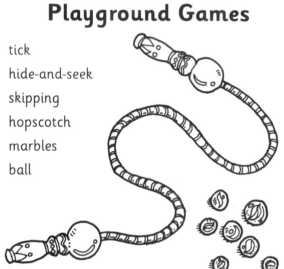

Books

stories
poems
mysteries
magic
adventure
information

Animals

cat
dog
gerbil
hamster
guinea pig
rabbit

Name: _____ Date: _____

| A | Explaining mathematical thinking |

Domino Discoveries

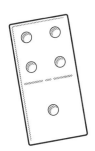

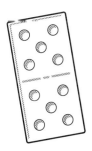

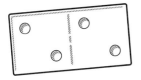
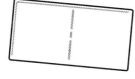
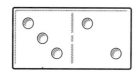
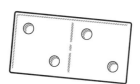

Name: _____ Date: _____

| B | Explaining mathematical thinking | C26 |

Dice Discoveries

Name: _____ Date: _____

| A | Using mathematical words | C27 |

above .... ❑	more .... ❑
add .... ❑	multiply........................... ❑
angle .... ❑	metric............................... ❑
behind............................. ❑	negative number .... ❑
block graph..................... ❑	next to .... ❑
calculation .... ❑	number .... ❑
capacity .... ❑	odd .... ❑
change .... ❑	order .... ❑
circle .... ❑	pattern .... ❑
cube .... ❑	pentagon .... ❑
cuboid............................. ❑	position .... ❑
curved .... ❑	predict............................. ❑
cylinder .... ❑	quarter .... ❑
data .... ❑	rectangle .... ❑
decimal .... ❑	reflective symmetry.......... ❑
digit .... ❑	right angle .... ❑
divide .... ❑	round .... ❑
double............................. ❑	rounding up/down .... ❑
enter and access .... ❑	shorter .... ❑
estimate .... ❑	shortest .... ❑
even .... ❑	smaller .... ❑
fewer.............................. ❑	smallest........................... ❑
flat .... ❑	sort .... ❑
frequency table .... ❑	sphere .... ❑
half .... ❑	square .... ❑
halving .... ❑	straight .... ❑
heavier .... ❑	subtract........................... ❑
heaviest .... ❑	symbol .... ❑
hexagon .... ❑	table .... ❑
inside .... ❑	the same .... ❑
interpret.......................... ❑	total................................ ❑
larger .... ❑	triangle .... ❑
largest............................. ❑	under .... ❑
longer .... ❑	unit .... ❑
longest .... ❑	weight.............................. ❑

Name: _____ Date: _____

B | Using mathematical words

C28

Maths words I know and use

– – – – – – – – – – cut along here and fold to make a concertina book – – – – – –

quarter ....
rectangle ....
reflective symmetry .....
right angle ....
round ....
rounding up/down ....
shorter ....
shortest ....
smaller ....
smallest ....
sort ....
sphere ....
square ....
straight ....
subtract ....
symbol ....
table ....
the same ....
total ....
triangle ....
under ....
unit ....
weight ....
whole number ....

half ....
halving ....
heavier ....
heaviest ....
hexagon ....
inside ....
interpret ....
larger ....
largest ....
length ....
longer ....
longest ....
more ....
multiply ....
metric ....
negative number ....
next to ....
number ....
odd ....
order ....
pattern ....
pentagon ....
position ....
predict ....

above ....
add ....
angle ....
behind ....
block graph ....
calculation ....
capacity ....
change ....
circle ....
cube ....
cuboid ....
curved ....
cylinder ....
data ....
decimal ....
digit ....
divide ....
double ....
enter and access ....
estimate ....
even ....
fewer ....
flat ....
frequency table ....

Name: _____ Date: _____

A | Interpret/construct pictograms

Clapometer readings for variety acts   = 2 minutes of clapping

= 1 minute of clapping

Magico the Magic Man

The Songbirds

Flea Circus

Jonny Juggler

Who is the most popular act? _____

How many minutes do the audience clap for
Flea Circus ? | minutes |

Which act is least popular? _____

• •

Find out how many children stay for
school dinners in each class   _____ day

Make a chart to show how many stay,
drawing one plate for each 10 children

classes	number of dinners

Name: _____ Date: _____

B | Interpret/construct pictograms

C30

Number of comics sold by the newsagent   📖 = 10 copies

📖 = 5 copies

Bluster

Zoe and Friends

The Gang

Jokey

[ ] copies of *Bluster* were sold

_____ is the most popular comic

The Gang is least popular [ ] copies were sold

• •

Find out how many children in each class are right-handed

Make a chart to show how many, drawing one hand for each 10 children

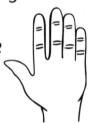

classes	number of right-handed children

| A | Find out by trying examples |

C31

Make patterns of squares – polyominoes

patterns of 2 squares

patterns of 3 squares

patterns of 4 squares

patterns of 5 squares

Name: _____ Date: _____

| B | Find out by trying examples |

Make patterns of triangles – triominoes

patterns of 2 triangles

patterns of 3 triangles

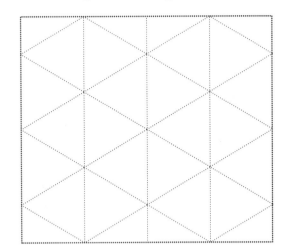

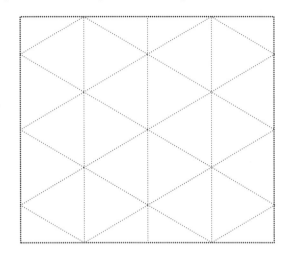

patterns of 4 triangles

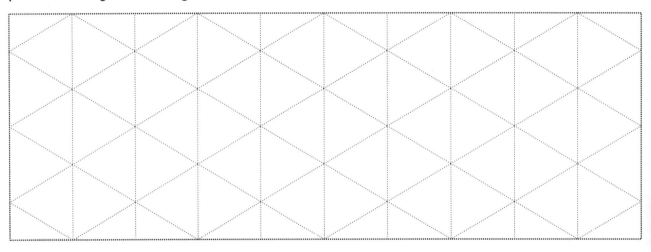

patterns of 5 triangles

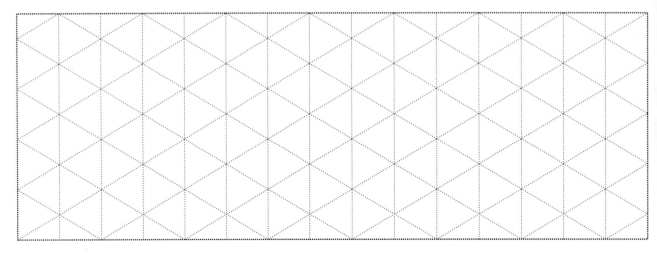

A Count, recognize, talk about numbers

Count how many

· ·

Point and read out in order

8 1 7 3 5
10 4 9 2 6

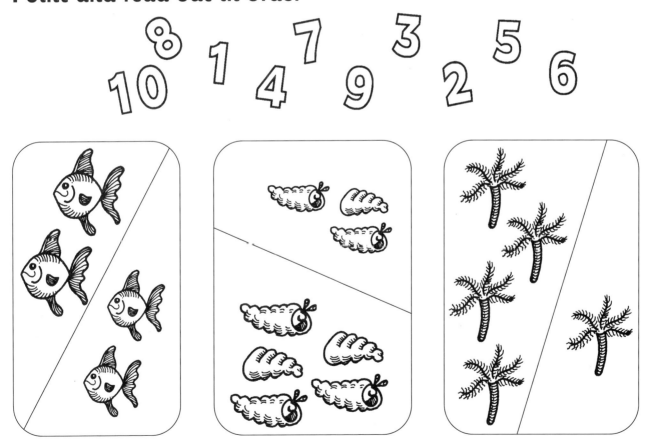

Number talk – more, most, less, fewer, smaller, larger, same as, least, largest, smallest

B Count, recognize, talk about numbers

Count how many

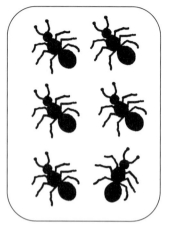

· ·

Point and read out in order

8   2   3   6   7   10   4   9   1   5

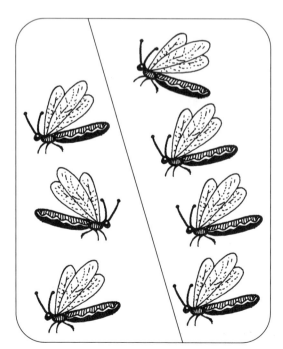

Number talk – more, most, less, fewer, smaller, larger, same as, least, largest, smallest

Name: _____ Date: _____

A | Count, read and write numbers   C35

Counts to 5 with confidence

| pencils |
| marbles |
| blocks |

Counts to 10 with confidence

Can write numerals   1 ☐   2 ☐   3 ☐   4 ☐   5 ☐

6 ☐   7 ☐   8 ☐   9 ☐   10 ☐

Can read number words one to five ☐   six to ten ☐

errors (write in)

_____

| one | two | three | four | five |
| six | seven | eight | nine | ten |

These can be cut out, mixed up and presented
to the child as flashcards

Name: _____ Date: _____

| B | Count, read and write numbers | C36 |

Counts to 5 with confidence

Counts to 10 with confidence

crayons
small balls
counting apparatus

Can write numerals   1 ☐   2 ☐   3 ☐   4 ☐   5 ☐

6 ☐   7 ☐   8 ☐   9 ☐   10 ☐

Can read number words one to five ☐   six to ten ☐

errors (write in)

_____

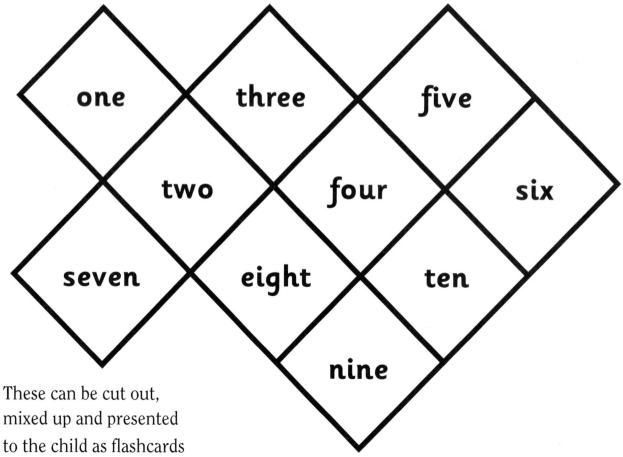

These can be cut out,
mixed up and presented
to the child as flashcards

Name: _____ Date: _____

| A | Add and subtract using a few objects | C37 |

Using   shells, conkers, books, marbles, small toys

Can do   addition to 5   ☐

subtraction to 5   ☐

Can do   addition to 10   ☐

subtraction to 10   ☐

Remarks

Name: _____ Date: _____

| B | Add and subtract using a few objects | C38 |

Using counting apparatus, crayons, paint brushes, fruit

Can do addition to 5 ☐

subtraction to 5 ☐

Can do addition to 10 ☐

subtraction to 10 ☐

• •

Remarks

Name: _____ Date: _____

| A | Repeating patterns |

Go on . . . .

Your patterns

Name: ______________________ Date: ____________

AT2 Level 1

B Repeating patterns

C40

Go on . . . . . .

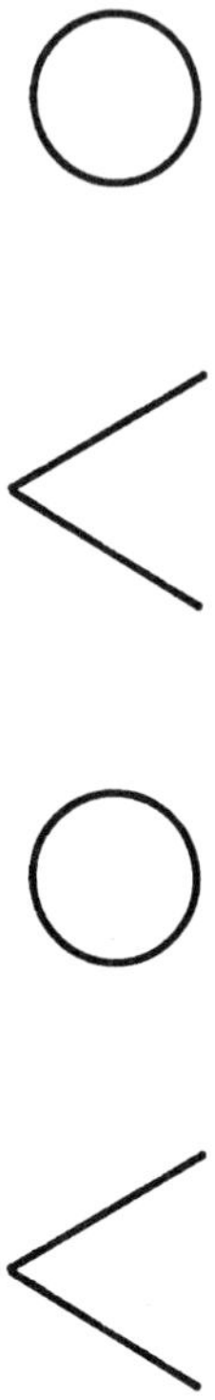

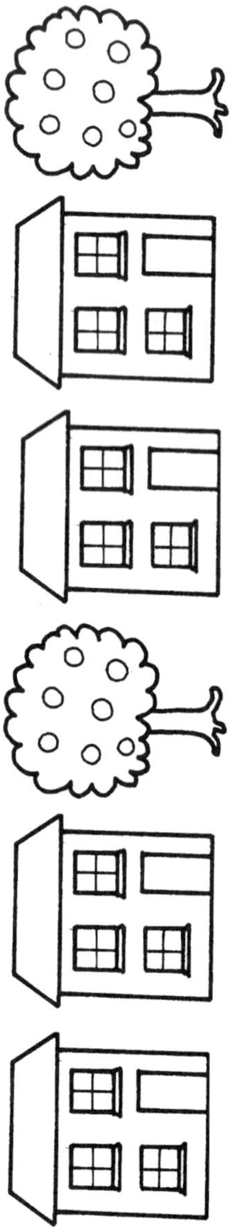

1 2 3 1 2 3

Your patterns

Name: _____ Date: _____

| A | Patterns in addition/subtraction to 10 | C41 |

Here are some ways of making 5, written so that they are in a pattern

5 + 0 = 5	10 – 5 = 5
4 + 1 = 5	9 – 4 = 5
3 + 2 = 5	8 – 3 = 5
2 + 3 = 5	7 – 2 = 5
1 + 4 = 5	6 – 1 = 5

Find two lots of ways of making 6

Set them down so that the number pattern shows

Find two lots of ways of making 7

Name: _____ Date: _____

| B | Patterns in addition/subtraction to 10 |

Here are some ways of making 5. Can you see the number pattern?

5 = 0 + 5	10 − 5 = 5
5 = 1 + 4	9 − 4 = 5
5 = 2 + 3	8 − 3 = 5
5 = 3 + 2	7 − 2 = 5
5 = 4 + 1	6 − 1 = 5
	5 − 0 = 5

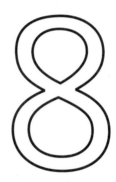

Find two lots of ways of making 8

Find two lots of ways of making 9

Name: _____ Date: _____

A │ Addition/subtraction facts to 10

Complete these snakes

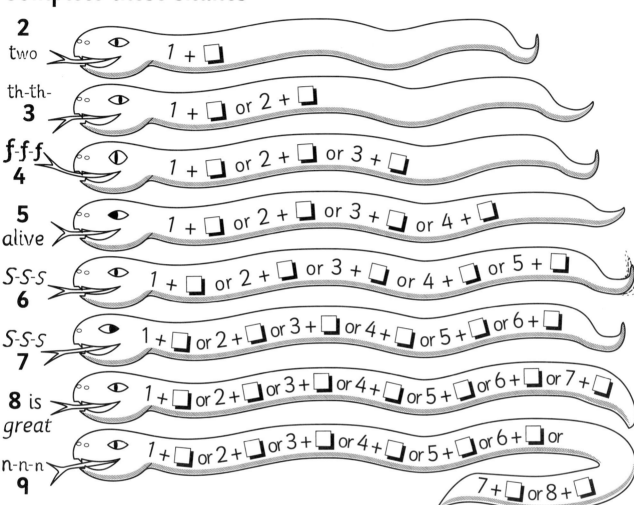

2
two — $1 + \square$

th-th-
3 — $1 + \square$ or $2 + \square$

f-f-f
4 — $1 + \square$ or $2 + \square$ or $3 + \square$

5
alive — $1 + \square$ or $2 + \square$ or $3 + \square$ or $4 + \square$

S-S-S
6 — $1 + \square$ or $2 + \square$ or $3 + \square$ or $4 + \square$ or $5 + \square$

S-S-S
7 — $1 + \square$ or $2 + \square$ or $3 + \square$ or $4 + \square$ or $5 + \square$ or $6 + \square$

8 is
great — $1 + \square$ or $2 + \square$ or $3 + \square$ or $4 + \square$ or $5 + \square$ or $6 + \square$ or $7 + \square$

n-n-n
9 — $1 + \square$ or $2 + \square$ or $3 + \square$ or $4 + \square$ or $5 + \square$ or $6 + \square$ or $7 + \square$ or $8 + \square$

Make 10

$1 +$	$= 10$	$10 - 1$	$=$
$2 +$	$= 10$	$10 - 2$	$=$
$3 +$	$= 10$	$10 - 3$	$=$
$4 +$	$= 10$	$10 - 4$	$=$
$5 +$	$= 10$	$10 - 5$	$=$
$6 +$	$= 10$	$10 - 6$	$=$
$7 +$	$= 10$	$10 - 7$	$=$
$8 +$	$= 10$	$10 - 8$	$=$
$9 +$	$= 10$	$10 - 9$	$=$

| B | Addition/subtraction facts to 10 | C44 |

Join the numbers that add together to make 10

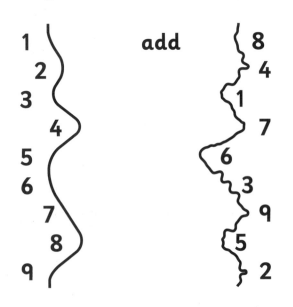

```
1            add        8
  2                     4
3                     1
    4                   7
5                     6
6                     3
    7                   9
    8                 5
9                     2
```

What do we take away from 10 to make these numbers?

9 is 10 –
8 is 10 –
7 is 10 –
6 is 10 –
5 is 10 –
4 is 10 –
3 is 10 –
2 is 10 –
1 is 10 –

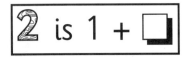

2 is 1 + ☐

3 is 1 + ☐ or 2 + ☐

join to make **5**   1   3   2   4

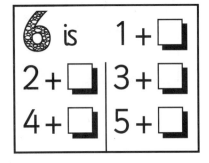

6 is   1 + ☐
2 + ☐ | 3 + ☐
4 + ☐ | 5 + ☐

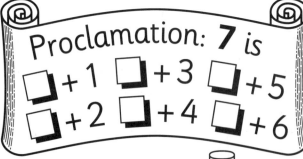

Proclamation: **7** is
☐ + 1   ☐ + 3   ☐ + 5
☐ + 2   ☐ + 4   ☐ + 6

Can you read this card?
4 is
1 + ☐
2 + ☐
3 + ☐

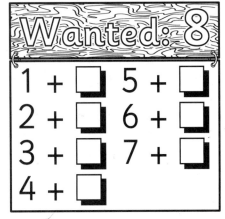

Wanted: 8
1 + ☐   5 + ☐
2 + ☐   6 + ☐
3 + ☐   7 + ☐
4 + ☐

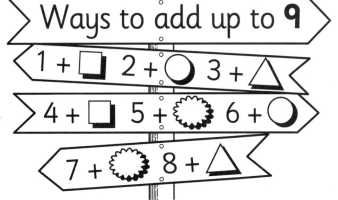

Ways to add up to **9**
1 + ☐   2 + ◐   3 + △
4 + ☐   5 + ✾   6 + ◐
7 + ✾   8 + △

Name: _____ Date: _____

AT2 Level 2

A Numbers to 100 and place value

C45

Put the numbers in order on the trucks

62   41   11   36
9   3   27   85   54

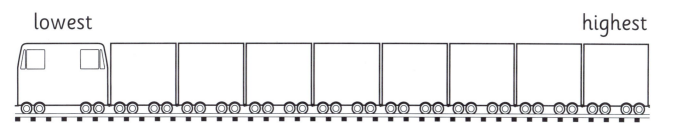

lowest   highest

....

Put these down as numerals

| eighty-one | seventeen | fifty-six |

| forty-four | twelve | ninety-seven |

....

How many tens are in these numbers?

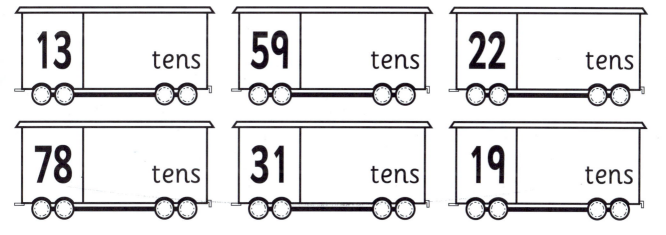

| 13 tens | 59 tens | 22 tens |
| 78 tens | 31 tens | 19 tens |

Name: _____ Date: _____

| B | Numbers to 100 and place value |

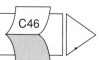
C46

Put the numbers in order on the buses

77   **13**   **85**   **41**

2   **9**   **48**   **23**   **92**

lowest number   highest number

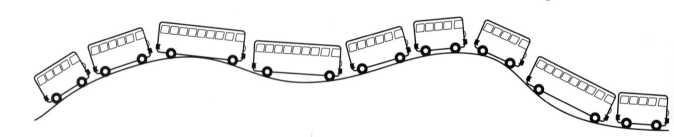

. . . .

Put these down in numerals

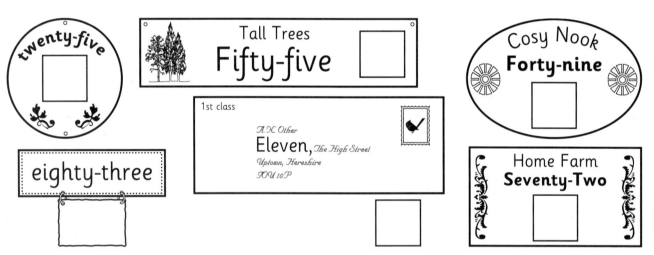

twenty-five

Tall Trees
Fifty-five

Cosy Nook
Forty-nine

eighty-three

1st class
A. N. Other
Eleven, The High Street
Uptown, Hereshire
YOU 10P

Home Farm
Seventy-Two

. . . .

How many tens are in these numbers?

33
tens

41
tens

66
tens

99
tens

18
tens

82
tens

57
tens

Name: _____ Date: _____

| A | Find the difference problems | C47 |

Problems

Class equipment	Addition	Subtraction
crayons		
books		
shoebags		
Number stories		
beans		
bears		

Shopping at a general store

    cost of 1 item

    cost of 2 items

    change from 10p

    change from 20p

Finding the difference

    to 10

    to 20

    more than 20

Name: _____ Date: _____

| B | Find the difference problems | C48 |

Problems

Class equipment	Addition	Subtraction
rulers		
erasers		
boxes		
Number stories		
pancakes		
pigs		

Shopping at a general store

cost of 1 item

cost of 2 items

change from 10p

change from 20p

Finding the difference

to 10

to 20

more than 20

Name: _____ Date: _____

A Missing number problems

What is missing?

5 + 2 = ☐   3 + 1 = ☐   7 + 3 = ☐

4 + ☐ = 6   2 + ☐ = 4   3 + ☐ = 9

7 − ☐ = 2   9 − ☐ = 1   10 − ☐ = 5

☐ + 2 = 3   ☐ + 1 = 9   ☐ + 5 = 8

☐ − 2 = 3   ☐ − 7 = 2   ☐ − 3 = 6

Use the numbers given to find what is missing

☐ + 1 = ☐   ☐ − 3 = ☐

5 + ☐ − ☐   7 − ☐ = ☐

☐ + ☐ = ☐   ☐ + ☐ = ☐

What numbers will you choose for these?

Name: _____ Date: _____

B | Missing number problems

C50

What is missing?

7 + 3 = ☐   2 + 2 = ☐   4 + 6 = ☐

3 + ☐ = 6   2 + ☐ = 7   4 + ☐ = 8

9 − ☐ = 2   5 − ☐ = 1   9 − ☐ = 5

☐ + 1 = 4   ☐ + 2 = 10   ☐ + 8 = 9

☐ − 3 = 2   ☐ − 5 = 2   ☐ − 4 = 5

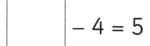

The clues to the missing numbers are on the page

☐ + 2 = ☐   ☐ − 1 = ☐

6 + ☐ = ☐   8 − ☐ = ☐

☐ + ☐ = ☐   ☐ + ☐ = ☐

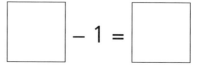

Do you enjoy inventing calculations?

Name: _____ Date: _____

| A | Halves and quarters |

Join each number to half of that number

4   2

2   1

10   3

8   4

6   5

Colour in half

Colour to match (the whole with the quarter)

Name: _____ Date: _____

| B | Halves and quarters |

C52

Join each number to half of that number

10   1

4   3

2   5

8   4

6   2

Colour in half

Colour to match (the whole with the quarter)

Name: _____ Date: _____

A │ Odds and evens

Colour the number track
odd numbers red, even numbers blue

Put stripes on the T-shirts with odd numbers

| 0 |
| 1 |
| 2 |
| 3 |
| 4 |
| 5 |
| 6 |
| 7 |
| 8 |
| 9 |
| 10 |
| 11 |
| 12 |
| 13 |
| 14 |
| 15 |
| 16 |
| 17 |
| 18 |
| 19 |
| 20 |

Look at the last digit and put a ✓ by even numbers

22 ✓   12   35

46   99   14

Name: _____ Date: _____

| B | Odds and evens | |

Join each number to the correct label – odd or even

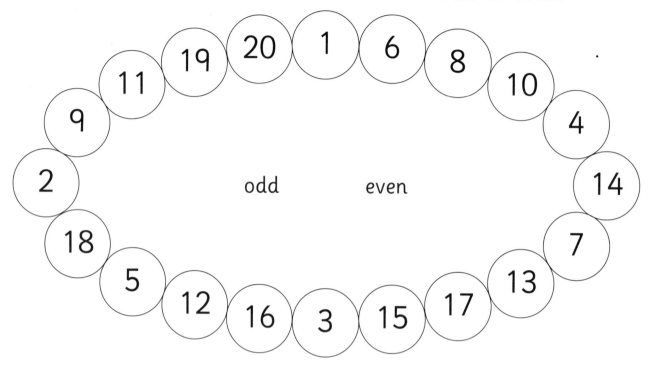

odd   even

Even numbers win a prize. Colour the lucky tickets

| 14 | 2 | 3 |

| 10 | 8 |

| 17 | 6 | 20 |

Look at the last digit and put a ✶ by odd numbers

31✶   7   26

15   49   12

Name: _____ Date: _____

A │ Interpreting big numbers

C55

How many **?**

36	3 tens

26		45		87	
302		563		129	

Make up some numbers for these

	4 tens		3 tens		1 ten
	6 tens		9 tens		0 tens

What do the 5s in these numbers mean?

Are they hundreds, tens or units?

15		250	
526		5	
45		58	
952		571	

Are you an expert on 10s?

I in 10d to be!

B | Interpreting big numbers   C56

How many **10**s

24   _2_ tens

48 __ tens   **72** __ tens   **19** __ tens

64 __ tens   **37** __ tens   **7** __ tens

How many **100**s ?

| 478 | 4 hundreds |

605		745	
838		296	
122		570	

Make up some numbers

Which is the biggest number here?

| 8 tens | 2 hundreds and 1 ten |

| 9 hundreds | 5 tens |

| 3 tens | 7 tens |

| 4 hundreds | 3 hundreds |

| A | Approximation |

C57

Approximate

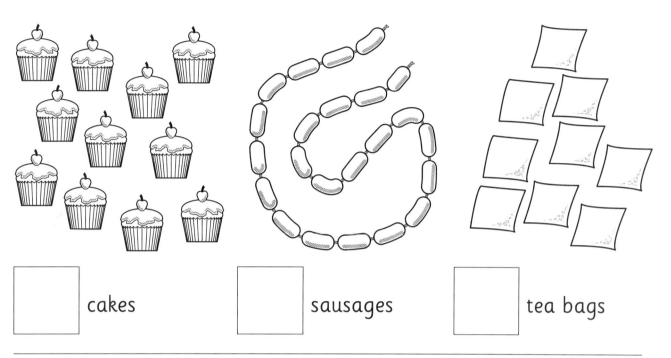

| | cakes | | sausages | | tea bags |

Round these up or down. What are they approximately?

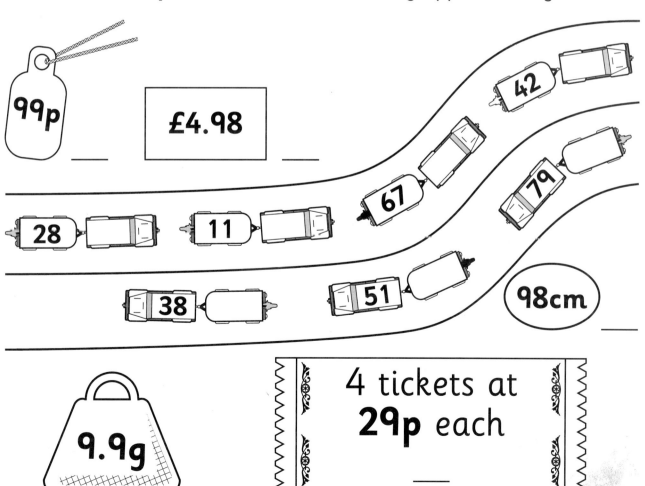

Name: _____ Date: _____

B | Approximation

Approximate

| apples | bags of oats | horseshoes |

Round these up or down. What are they approximately?

horse treat
19p
____

hay bale
____ **£2.98**

£150.99

_____

999g
Oats
____

horse pictures
4 at **9p** each _____

29   78   89   51

A │ Decimal money

hat box
£1.95

garden hat
£20.15

clown hat
£10.50

cloche
£5.65

feather hat
£8.99

top hat
£35.50

veil hat
£15.30

beret
£1.75

flowers 35p

feathers
65p

veils £1.15

Shop for these and work out the totals

1 hat box and 1 garden hat

1 cloche and 2 flowers

4 feathers and 2 berets

1 top hat and 2 hat boxes

How much change from £10 if I buy these?

1 feather hat

3 berets

1 cloche hat

4 hat boxes

List some prices which will total almost

£20   _ _ _ _ _ _

what is bought   _ _ _ _ _ _

_ _ _ _ _ _

Total _____

£40   _ _ _ _ _ _

what is bought   _ _ _ _ _ _

_ _ _ _ _ _

Total _____

Name: _____ Date: _____

| B | Decimal Money | C60 ▷ |

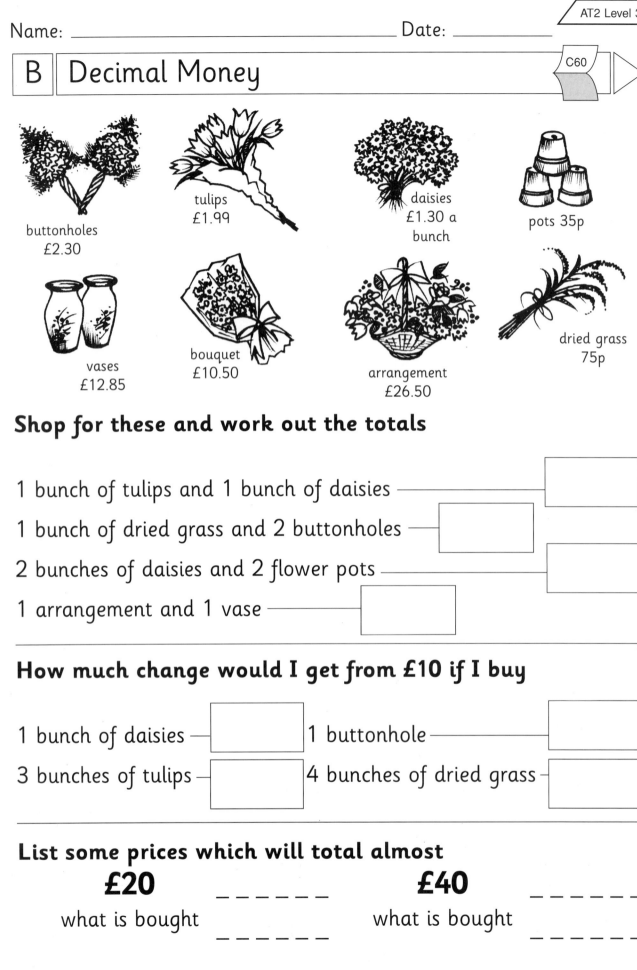

buttonholes
£2.30

tulips
£1.99

daisies
£1.30 a
bunch

pots 35p

vases
£12.85

bouquet
£10.50

arrangement
£26.50

dried grass
75p

Shop for these and work out the totals

1 bunch of tulips and 1 bunch of daisies ⸻

1 bunch of dried grass and 2 buttonholes ⸻

2 bunches of daisies and 2 flower pots ⸻

1 arrangement and 1 vase ⸻

How much change would I get from £10 if I buy

1 bunch of daisies ⸺ [ ]   1 buttonhole ⸻ [ ]

3 bunches of tulips ⸺ [ ]   4 bunches of dried grass ⸺ [ ]

List some prices which will total almost

£20 _ _ _ _ _ _   ### £40 _ _ _ _ _ _

what is bought   what is bought

_ _ _ _ _ _   _ _ _ _ _ _

_ _ _ _ _ _   _ _ _ _ _ _

Total _____   Total _____

Name: _____ Date: _____

| A | Negative numbers |

Complete the number line

Tick the temperature on a really cold day

10 °C　　　　**15 °C**　　　　**–2 °C**

Tick what temperature might be in the freezer

2 °C　　　　**–10 °C**　　　　**10 °C**

Make a negative number show on a calculator
and show your teacher

Find out the temperature in the coldest
part of the world. Write in the temperature
and the place name here

_____

What happens when you add together –2 and –4?
Use a calculator to help you.
What do you notice about the answer?

10
9
8
7
6
5
4
3
2
1
0

Name: _____ Date: _____

B ∥ Negative numbers

Complete the number line

Tick the temperature of a day when puddles freeze over

–4 °C   **12 °C**   **40 °C**

Tick which temperature you should keep your ice lollies at

10 °C   **8 °C**   **–5 °C**

Make a negative number show on a calculator and show your teacher

Draw the scale on a maximum and minimum thermometer here

10
9
8
7
6
5
4
3
2
1
0

Name: _____ Date: _____

| A | Add and subtract to 20 including 0 | C63 |

11 + 3 =

16 + 4 =

18 + 1 =

19 + 1 =

12 + 6 =

17 + 2 =

13 + 5 =

Are you quick and careful at doing these?

17 – 5 =

19 – 8 =

20 – 0 =

12 – 2 =

13 – 1 =

15 – 4 =

14 – 0 =

---

15 +   = 18

20 +   = 20

13 +   = 16

18 +   = 20

17 +   = 19

14 +   = 17

16 +   = 20

What is missing here?

16 –   = 11

14 –   = 10

18 –   = 13

20 –   = 17

13 –   = 10

15 –   = 13

17 –   = 12

＋ 12 = 19

＋ 19 = 19

＋ 15 = 17

＋ 14 = 18

＋ 16 = 20

＋ 20 = 20

＋ 13 = 15

－ 9 = 10

－ 1 = 13

－ 7 = 12

－ 6 = 14

－ 3 = 17

－ 5 = 11

－ 2 = 14

B | **Add and subtract to 20 including 0**

C64

18 + 1 =

14 + 4 =

11 + 6 =

13 + 5 =

16 + 3 =

17 + 2 =

19 + 0 =

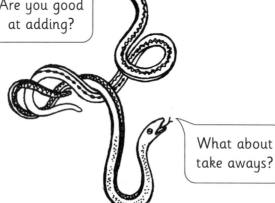

Are you good at adding?

What about take aways?

20 – 10 =

11 – 0 =

13 – 2 =

16 – 4 =

18 – 6 =

17 – 5 =

14 – 2 =

---

16 +   = 19

18 +   = 19

13 +   = 18

20 +   = 20

11 +   = 19

14 +   = 17

12 +   = 15

19 –   = 12

13 –   = 11

14 –   = 10

17 –   = 16

18 –   = 13

12 –   = 11

20 –   = 20

   + 14 = 18

   + 16 = 20

   + 11 = 12

   + 13 = 17

   + 19 = 19

   + 12 = 15

   + 10 = 20

Think carefully. Don't tie yourself in knots!

   – 3 = 14

   – 9 = 11

   – 0 = 15

   – 7 = 12

   – 4 = 15

   – 2 = 10

   – 1 = 18

Name: _____ Date: _____

| **A** | 2, 5, 10 x tables and up to 5 x 5 | C65 |

2 2 2 2 2   5   5   5   5   5

10   10   10   10

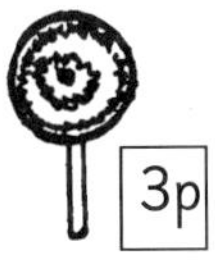

3 cost ☐ p

5 cost ☐ p

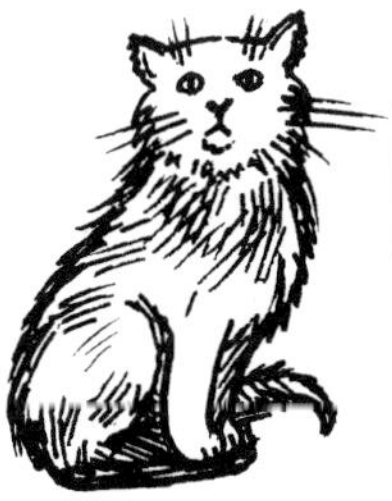

3p

☐ cats have 12 legs

☐ legs on 2 cats

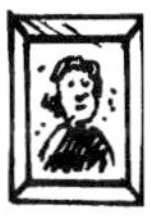

☐ corners on 4 pictures

20 corners on ☐ pictures

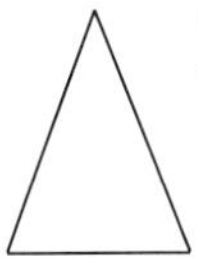

2 triangles have ☐ sides

12 sides on ☐ triangles

Name: ______________________ Date: ____________

AT2 Level 3

B 2, 5, 10 x tables and up to 5 x 5

C66

2 2 2 2 2

5 5 5 5 5

10 10 10 10

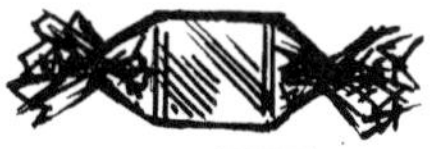

3p

4 cost ☐ p

2 cost ☐ p

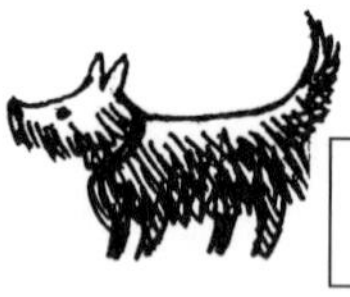

☐ dogs have 16 legs

☐ legs on 3 dogs

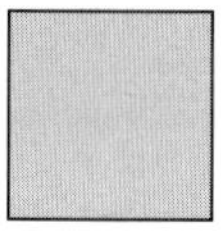

☐ corners on 5 squares

8 corners on ☐ squares

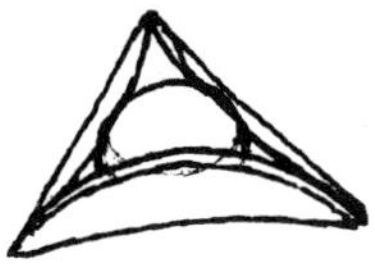

3 cornered (tricorne) hat

3 hats have ☐ corne

15 corners on ☐ hat

Name: _____ Date: _____

A	Division by 2, 5 and 10

C67

Colour in the traffic light numbers
(Some numbers will need to be more than one colour)

red
can be divided
by 2

amber
can be divided
by 5

green
can be divided
by 10

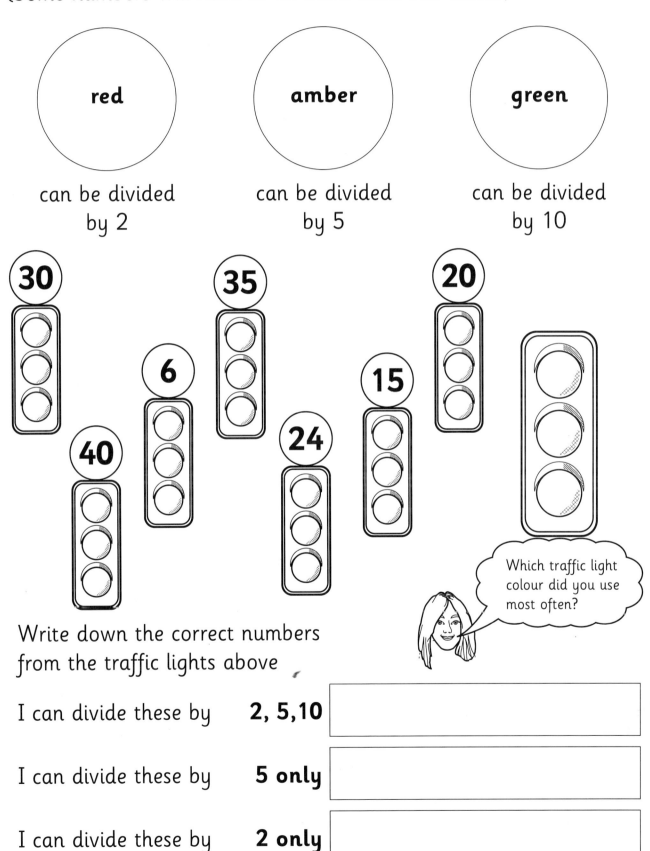

Write down the correct numbers
from the traffic lights above

I can divide these by   **2, 5, 10** [   ]

I can divide these by   **5 only**   [   ]

I can divide these by   **2 only**   [   ]

Which traffic light colour did you use most often?

Name: _____ Date: _____

B | Division by 2, 5 and 10 | C68

Colour in the autumn leaves
(Some leaves will be more than one colour)

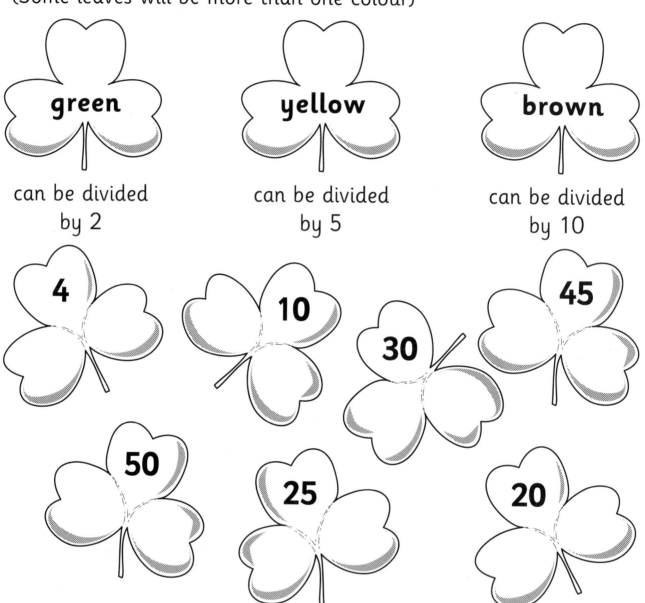

green can be divided by 2

yellow can be divided by 5

brown can be divided by 10

4   10   45   30   50   25   20

Write down the correct numbers
from the leaves above

I can divide these by **2, 5, 10** [   ]

I can divide these by **5 only** [   ]

I can divide these by **2 only** [   ]

Name: _____ Date: _____

| A | Multiplication and division problems |

C69

In what ways can these marbles be put into equal groups?

How much do
3 of these
pencil cases
cost?

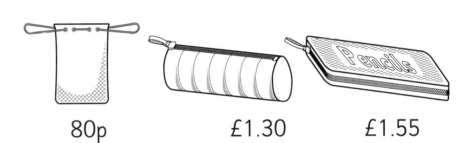

80p   £1.30   £1.55

3   3   3

of these cost   of these cost   of these cost

_____   _____   _____

How many
of them
could you
buy with £4?

£4   £4   £4

buys this many   buys this many   buys this many
of this sort   of this sort   of this sort

_____   _____   _____

In what ways
can these pencils
be shared equally?

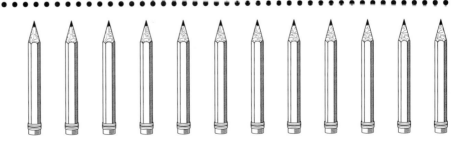

Name: _____ Date: _____

| B | Multiplication and division problems | C70 |

In what ways can these eggs be shared out?

Feed is £1.25 for a small bag. Chicks cost 45p each. Chicken wire is £1.80 for 1 metre

£1.25

45p

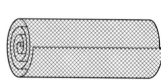

£1.80 per m

4

bags cost

_____

4

chicks cost

_____

4

metres of wire cost

_____

What could you buy for £5?

£5

buys this much feed

_____

£5

buys this many chicks

_____

£5

buys this much wire

_____

Here are 20 feeding dishes
In what ways can these be shared between chicks?

Name: _____ Date: _____

A | Remainders

Find the remainder

$6 \div 5 =$

$10 \div 4 =$

$12 \div 5 =$

$13 \div 2 =$

$20 \div 3 =$

$15 \div 6 =$

$25 \div 7 =$

$30 \div 4 =$

$15 \div 10 =$

$3 \div 2 =$

Did you get them all right?

| B | Remainders |

C72

Find the remainder

$7 \div 5 =$

$4 \div 4 =$

$14 \div 4 =$

$15 \div 2 =$

$17 \div 5 =$

$19 \div 3 =$

$11 \div 2 =$

$30 \div 7 =$

$4 \div 3 =$

$6 \div 5 =$

Do you like finding remainders?

Name: _____ Date: _____

Name: _____ Date: _____

| A | Using a calculator |

C73

Use a calculator to find the answers. Write them in.

1 259 + 277 = [ ]
2 375 + 519 = [ ]
3 393 + 213 = [ ]
4 141 + 88 = [ ]
5 404 + 338 = [ ]

6 615 + 527 = [ ]
7 446 + 115 = [ ]
8 624 + 327 = [ ]
9 49 + 259 = [ ]
10 243 + 481 = [ ]

11 195 – 81 = [ ]
12 171 – 63 = [ ]
13 435 – 147 = [ ]
14 489 – 211 = [ ]
15 698 – 197 = [ ]

16 622 – 43 = [ ]
17 536 – 375 = [ ]
18 916 – 403 = [ ]
19 933 – 319 = [ ]
20 539 – 66 = [ ]

21 69 × 33 = [ ]
22 21 × 42 = [ ]
23 97 × 4 = [ ]
24 121 × 59 = [ ]
25 22 × 103 = [ ]

26 45 × 87 = [ ]
27 145 × 53 = [ ]
28 17 × 141 = [ ]
29 277 × 4 = [ ]
30 417 × 2 = [ ]

31 325 ÷ 13 = [ ]
32 49 ÷ 9 = [ ]
33 101 ÷ 24 = [ ]
34 671 ÷ 36 = [ ]
35 704 ÷ 57 = [ ]

36 756 ÷ 102 = [ ]
37 649 ÷ 67 = [ ]
38 185 ÷ 85 = [ ]
39 712 ÷ 13 = [ ]
40 225 ÷ 18 = [ ]

Name: _____ Date: _____

| B | Using a calculator | C74 |

Use a calculator to find the answers. Write them in.

1 $523 + 913 =$ ☐

2 $760 + 239 =$ ☐

3 $463 + 793 =$ ☐

4 $602 + 684 =$ ☐

5 $263 + 577 =$ ☐

6 $231 + 62 \ \ =$ ☐

7 $411 + 79 \ \ =$ ☐

8 $32 + 761 \ \ =$ ☐

9 $827 + 13 \ \ =$ ☐

10 $319 + 109 =$ ☐

11 $471 - 19 \ \ =$ ☐

12 $893 - 57 \ \ =$ ☐

13 $529 - 151 =$ ☐

14 $955 - 311 =$ ☐

15 $399 - 141 =$ ☐

16 $917 - 891 =$ ☐

17 $402 - 217 =$ ☐

18 $189 - 59 \ \ =$ ☐

19 $96 - 37 \ \ =$ ☐

20 $80 - 17 \ \ =$ ☐

21 $84 \times 109 \ \ =$ ☐

22 $71 \times 67 \ \ =$ ☐

23 $157 \times 59 \ \ =$ ☐

24 $198 \times 113 =$ ☐

25 $603 \times 99 \ \ =$ ☐

26 $702 \times 47 \ \ =$ ☐

27 $79 \times 79 \ \ =$ ☐

28 $27 \times 143 \ \ =$ ☐

29 $60 \times 83 \ \ =$ ☐

30 $340 \times 4 \ \ =$ ☐

31 $181 \div 14 \ \ =$ ☐

32 $642 \div 17 \ \ =$ ☐

33 $776 \div 36 \ \ =$ ☐

34 $700 \div 202 =$ ☐

35 $37 \div 17 \ \ =$ ☐

36 $391 \div 131 =$ ☐

37 $857 \div 269 =$ ☐

38 $572 \div 95 \ \ =$ ☐

39 $883 \div 73 \ \ =$ ☐

40 $438 \div 19 \ \ =$ ☐

Name: _____ Date: _____

A | Mental computation strategies

C75

Finish the patterns

Looking for patterns helps in number work.

0, 2, 4, 6, —, —, —, —, —, —, —

1 + 3 = 5, 3 + 5 = , 5 + 7 = , _____

12,   22,   32, —, —, —, —, —, —

....

How are these patterns made?

0,   5,   10,   15,   20

_____

95,   80,   65,   50,   35

....

Write down how you do these calculations.

| 51 + 28 | 72 – 41 |

Name: _____ Date: _____

B | Mental computation strategies

C76

Finish the patterns

Be a pattern spotter. It makes you good at number work.

0, 1, 3, 5, 7, ___, ___, ___, ___, ___, ___

2 + 4 = 6, 4 + 6 =   , _____

27, 32, 37, 42, ___ , ___ , ___ , ___

. . . .

How are these patterns made?

1, 2 , 4, 8, 16

_____

49, 39, 29, 19, 9

. . . .

Write down how you do these calculations.

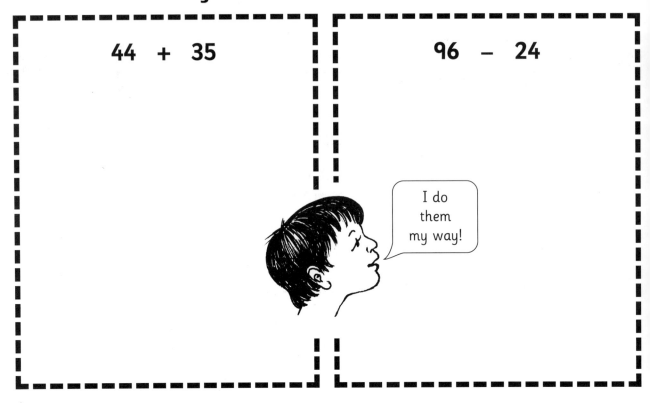

44 + 35

96 – 24

I do them my way!

Name: _____ Date: _____

A Function machines

Fantastic Frankie

What comes out?

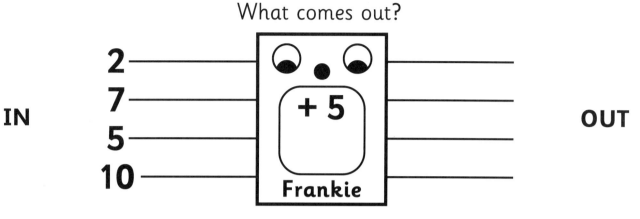

IN — 2, 7, 5, 10 → **+ 5** (Frankie) → OUT

What is the output?

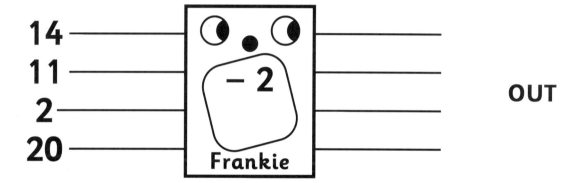

IN — 14, 11, 2, 20 → **− 2** (Frankie) → OUT

What is Frankie doing?

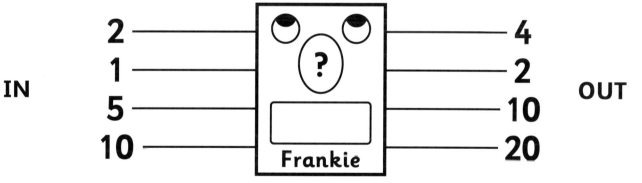

IN — 2, 1, 5, 10 → **?** (Frankie) → OUT — 4, 2, 10, 20

What operation is in Frankie?

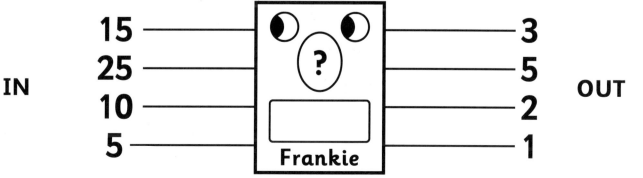

IN — 15, 25, 10, 5 → **?** (Frankie) → OUT — 3, 5, 2, 1

Name: _____ Date: _____

| B | Function machines |

Electronic Cat

What comes out?

IN — 1, 3, 7, 10 — **+ 7** — OUT

What is the output?

IN — 5, 9, 14, 20 — **– 4** — OUT

What is cat doing?

IN — 2, 1, 4, 10 — OUT — 6, 3, 12, 30

What is cat's operation here?

IN — 6, 10, 20, 4 — OUT — 3, 5, 10, 2

A ‖ Shape talk

Can:

    sort 3-D shapes ....❏

    sort 2-D shapes ....❏

Words used in sorting:

    straight   other words used
    flat
    curved
    round
    pointed

• •

Using Lego®/other apparatus:

    made a model of

    words used in talking about model

Name: _____ Date: _____

| B | Shape talk | C80 |

Can:

sort 3-D shapes ....❏

sort 2-D shapes ....❏

Words used in sorting:

straight   other words used
flat
curved
round
pointed

• •

Using straws and links or Plasticine®:

made a model of

words used in talking about model

Name: _____ Date: _____

| A | Position words |

slipper

Say where the slipper is

Name: _____ Date: _____

| B | Position words |

Say where the beetle is

 beetle

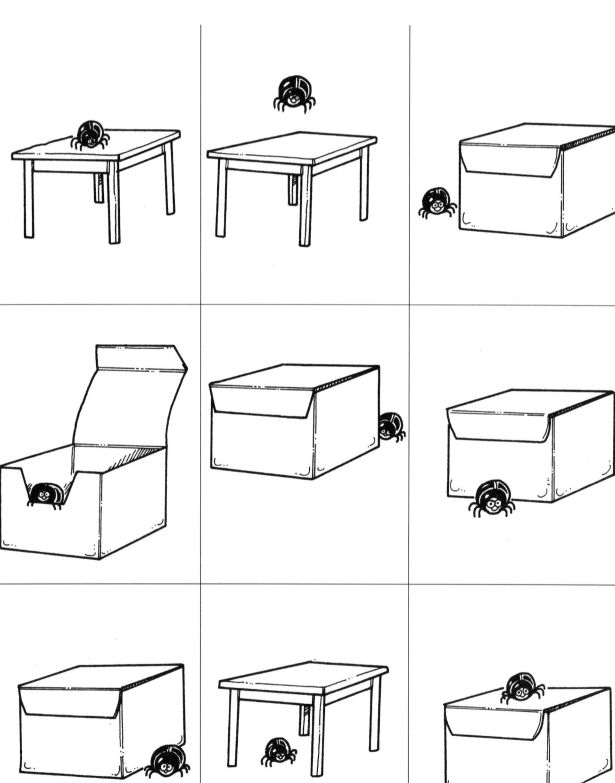

Name: _____ Date: _____

| A | Compare and order objects and events | C83 |

pencils

friends

food packs

things I do

Name: _____ Date: _____

B Compare and order objects and events   C84

crayons

buildings

snacks

things I do

Name: _____ Date: _____

| A | Common 2-D and 3-D shapes | C85 |

Join up the shape to its name

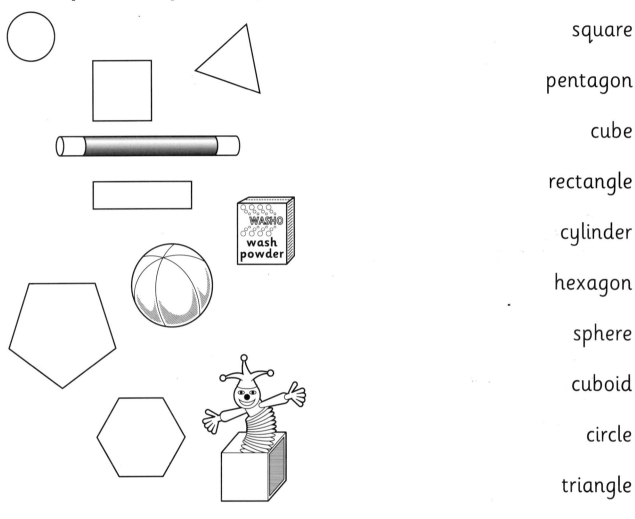

square

pentagon

cube

rectangle

cylinder

hexagon

sphere

cuboid

circle

triangle

Name these shapes

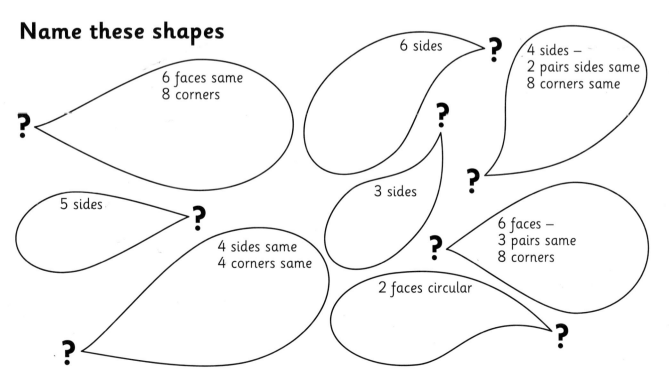

6 faces same
8 corners

6 sides

4 sides –
2 pairs sides same
8 corners same

5 sides

3 sides

4 sides same
4 corners same

6 faces –
3 pairs same
8 corners

2 faces circular

Name: _____ Date: _____

| B | Common 2-D and 3-D shapes |

Join up the shape to its name

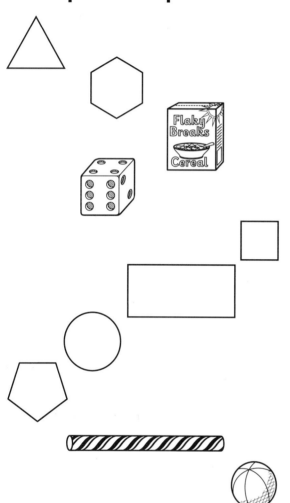

cuboid

square

pentagon

rectangle

cube

circle

cylinder

triangle

hexagon

sphere

Name these shapes

4 sides same 4 corners same ▼	5 sides ▼	6 faces same 8 corners ▼
3 sides ▼	2 faces circular ▼	6 faces (3 pairs) 8 corners same ▼
	4 sides (2 pairs) 4 corners same ▼	6 sides ▼

Name: _____ Date: _____

A	Types of movement

MOVEMENT LESSON RECORD

Theme: robots

Session 1

Can move in straight lines using whole body (translation) ....❑

Can rotate whole body (turn right around) ....❑

Session 2

Can turn whole body as robot through a right angle ....❑

Can repeat this movement turning through 1, 2, 3, 4 right angles ....❑

Session 3

Can mobilize parts of the body to show angles ....❑

Can invent a robot routine to show right-angle turns and
angles in parts of the robot ....❑

Session 4

Can respond to instructions to turn right or left as robot ....❑

Can add these to the robot routine ....❑

B | Types of movement

MOVEMENT LESSON RECORD

Theme: maze puzzle

Session 1

Can move whole body in straight lines to 'go for a walk' (translation)............❑

Can turn whole body (rotate)...❑

Session 2

Can turn right angles ....❑

Can take a walk through an imaginary maze turning through
1, 2, 3, 4 right angles...❑

Session 3

Can show angles with parts of the body as they move around the maze ....❑

Can invent a maze traversal 'routine' and story...❑

Session 4

Can turn left and right in an imaginary maze devised by the teacher................❑

Can develop a maze routine using left and right instructions ....❑

Name: _____ Date: _____

A | Right angles

Put ⌐ **in where there are right angles**

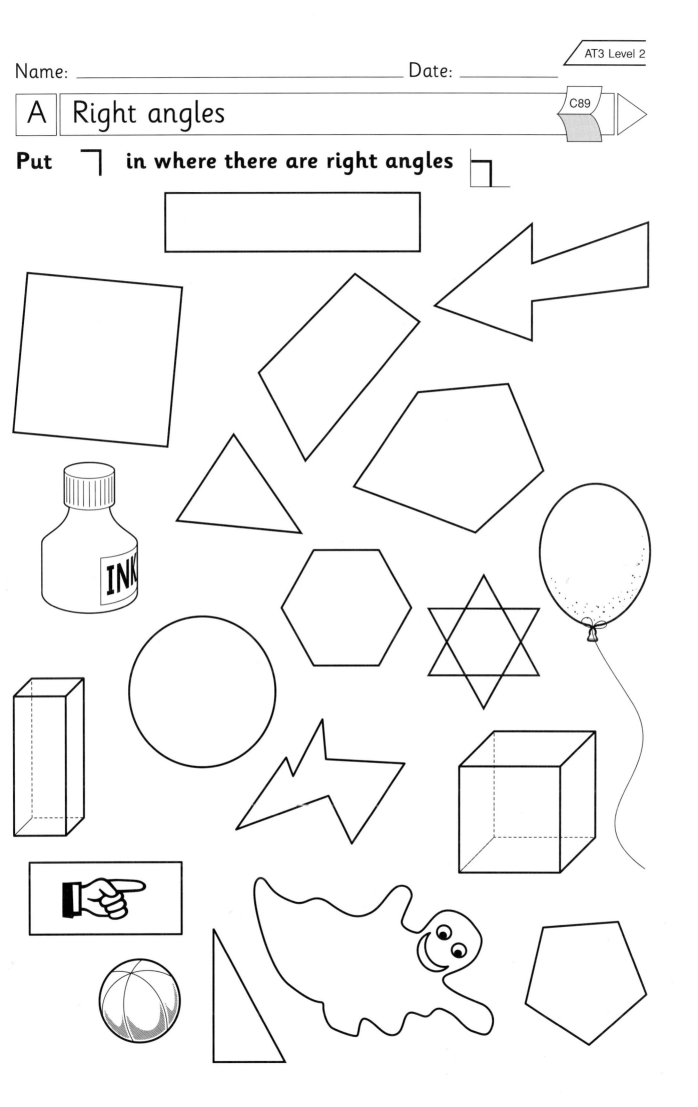

B Right angles

C90

Put ⌐ **in where there are right angles**

Name: _____ Date: _____

| A | Non-standard measures: length and mass | C91 |

I have used: **to measure:**

 span

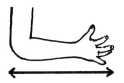 cubit

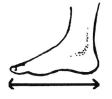 foot

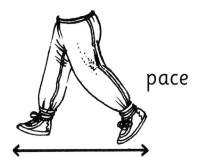 pace

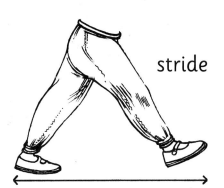 stride

things for weighing

B | Non-standard measures: length and mass

C92

Write or draw what you measured with these

span

cubit

foot

stride

pace

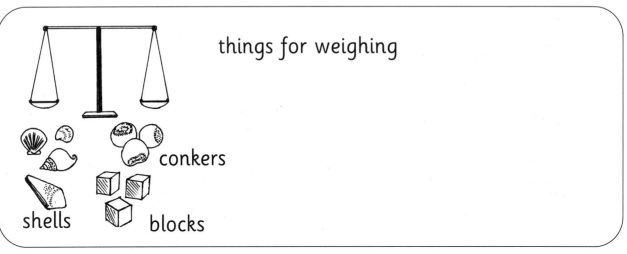

things for weighing

conkers

shells   blocks

Name: _____ Date: _____

| A | Standard measures: length and mass |

Are these measures of length or mass?
Write in length or mass by each measure

pound	mass	mile	
foot		inch	
yard		kilogram	
ounce		centimetre	
gram		metre	

By each picture write in
which measure you would use

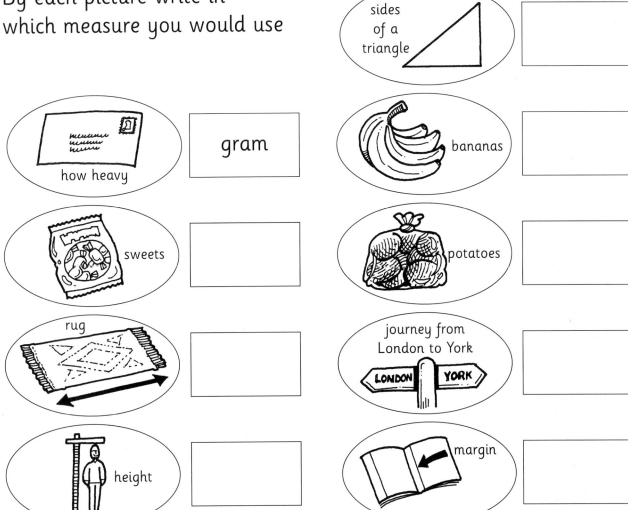

sides of a triangle

how heavy   gram

bananas

sweets

potatoes

rug

journey from London to York

LONDON   YORK

height

margin

Name: _____ Date: _____

B | Standard measures: length and mass   C94

Are these measures of length or mass?
Write in length or mass by each measure

pound	mass	metre	
yard		foot	
inch		mile	
ounce		gram	
kilogram		centimetre	

By each picture write in
which measure you would use

sides of a square [ ]

choc bar — gram

table [ ]

motorway [ ]

potting compost [ ]

parcel [ ]

cereal [ ]

How much does he weigh? [ ]

plums [ ]

Name: _____ Date: _____

| A | Sorting shapes |

Sorts according to criteria using card shapes and packaging

Sort	Explanation given
1	
2	
3	
4	
5	

Can identify criteria used in sorts done by the teacher or by other children

Sort	Criteria described
1	
2	
3	
4	
5	

Name: _____ Date: _____

| B | Sorting shapes |

Sorts according to criteria using bought-in geometric shapes and mathematically accurate 3-D shapes

Sort	Explanation given
1	
2	
3	
4	
5	

Can identify criteria used in sorts done by the teacher or by other children

Sort	Criteria described
1	
2	
3	
4	
5	

Name: _____ Date: _____

A Reflective symmetry

Put a ring around the things that show reflective or
mirror symmetry
Draw in where there are some lines and planes of symmetry

Name: _____ Date: _____

B	Reflective symmetry

Put a ring around the things that show reflective or
mirror symmetry
Draw in where there are some lines and planes of symmetry

Name: _____ Date: _____

| A | Length, capacity, mass, time (NSU) |

C99

Use these to measure things in your classroom
Draw what you measure and write in your findings

	draw here	write results
 cups, pots, bowls		
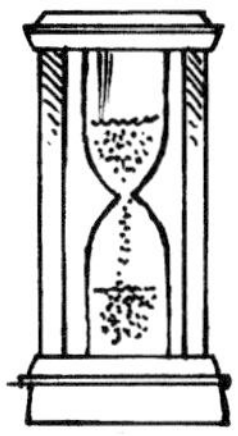 sand timer or water timer		
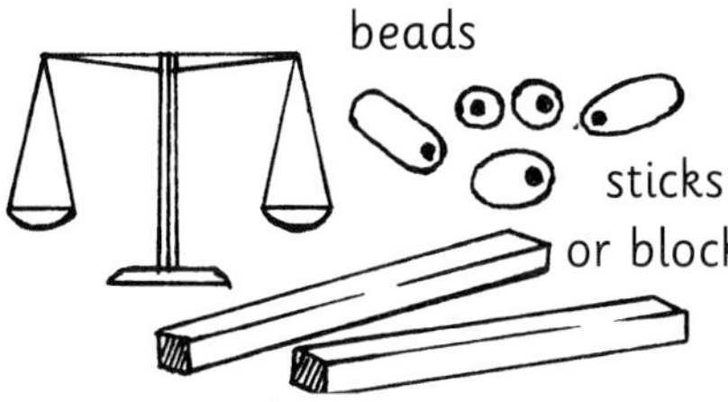 beads sticks or blocks		
 handspan		
 stride		
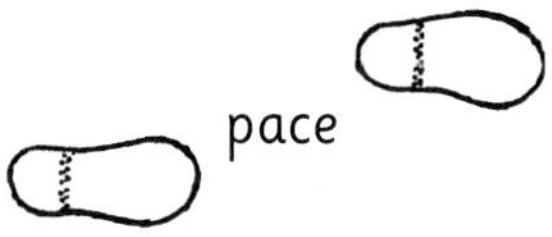 pace		
 foot		
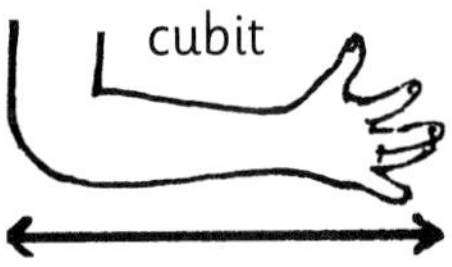 cubit		

Name: _____ Date: _____

| B | Length, capacity, mass, time (NSU) |

Use these to measure things in your classroom
Draw what you measure and write in your findings

	draw here write results
cups, jugs, bowls	
sand timer or water timer	
balance, shells, pasta	
handspan, finger, foot, pace, stride	

Name: _____ Date: _____

A │ Length, capacity, mass and time (SU)

Join each picture to the correct measure

Look carefully first and use a different coloured pencil each time

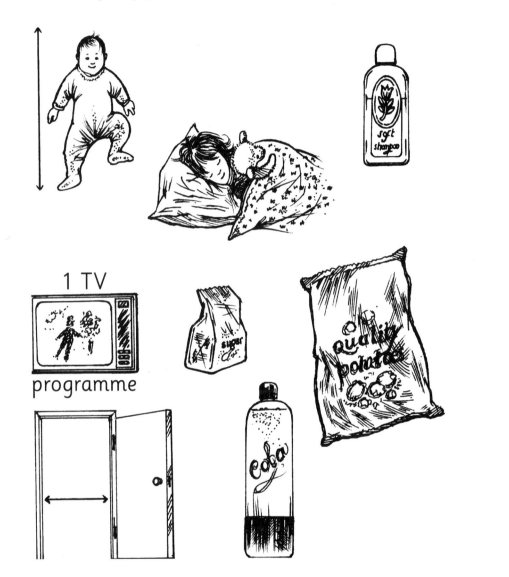

50 cm

500 ml

2 litres

1 TV

1 m

programme

¹/₂ kilo

15 minutes

8 hours

The quantity of water to make
squash for ten people

5 kg

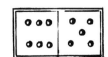

half an hour

How long playing dominoes

1 litre

Name: _____ Date: _____

B | Length, capacity, mass and time (SU) C102

Join each picture to the correct measure
Look carefully first and use a different coloured pencil each time

To have lunch

Assembly

half an hour

2 litres

1 m

1 l

60 cm

500 ml

20 minutes

The quantity of water to make tea
for all the teachers?

1 hour

1 kg

How long playing
a computer game

$^1/_2$ kilo

Record Sheet 1 Class Record

ass	Level		Date	
			Teacher's name	
me		AT1	AT2	AT3

Record Sheet 2 Child's Record

Name		Date of birth	Teacher's Initials

Level 1

AT1	Date	AT2	Date	AT3	Date
1 Prac Maths		1 Count/talk numbers		1 Shape talk	
2 Objects		2 Count, read, write		2 Position words	
3 Using Patterns		3 Add, subtract		3 Compare and order	
		4 Repeating Patterns			

Level 2

AT1	Date	AT2	Date	AT3	Date
4 Tools/maths		5 Add/subtract patterns		4 2-D/3-D shapes	
5 Talk about maths		6 Add/subtract facts		5 Movement	
6 Maths lang		7 Numbers to 100		6 Right angles	
7 Block graph		8 Find difference		7 NSU length/mass	
8 Predict		9 Missing numbers		8 SU length/mass	
9 What if?		10 Halves/quarters			
		11 Odds/evens			

Level 3

AT1	Date	AT2	Date	AT3	Date
10 Problem solving		12 Big numbers		9 Sorting shapes	
11 Organizing/checking		13 Approximations		10 Reflective symmetry	
12 Explaining		14 Decimal money		11 Non-standard measures	
13 Maths words		15 Negative numbers		12 Metric measures	
14 Pictogram		16 Add/subtract to 20			
15 Find out		17 2, 5, 10 x tables			
		18 Divide by 2, 5, 10			
		19 Multiply/divide			
		20 Remainders			
		21 Calculators			
		22 Mental computation			
		23 Function machines			